MW01469211

Shame Shame Go Away!

Confessions of a Little Dutch Girl

By Anika Lyn Grace

Shame, Shame, Go Away!

All rights reserved. No part of this book may be reproduced or transmitted in any form or by any means without written permission of the author.

Some names and identifying details in this memoir have been changed to protect the privacy of individuals. I have tried to recreate events, locales and conversations from my memories of them. In order to maintain their anonymity of individuals and places, I may have changed some identifying characteristics and details such as physical properties, occupations and places of residence.

Copyright © 2012 by Anika Lyn Grace

ISBN 978-0-9848542-4-0

Cover Illustration Copyright © 2012 by Jacob Kubon
Cover design by Jacob Kubon
Book design and production by Splattered Ink Press
www.splatteredinkpress.com

Grateful to God for empowering me with courage, I share my life's spiritual journey. With my memoir, I claim the hidden feelings of my heart, previously demeaned, ignored, or threatened. God intended me to heal, so my life story may encourage, empower, and enlighten others. Gaining my voice I became free as I accept and love myself. My hope and my prayer is that others may be inspired to claim the freedom of their voice as well.

Acknowledgments

To those who encouraged me to write,
  Listened as I sought words to express my feelings,
    Insisted that I continue when I wanted to give up
      To accomplish my dream of completing my memoir:

THANK YOU WITH ALL MY HEART!

Table of Contents

Where Are You, God? 1
The Perfect Middle Child 5
The Little Dutch Girl Loved Church 12
Falling In Love 16
Lord, For My Mother, Give Me Someone to Date 19
The Chapel Wedding 24
Will You Please Forgive Me? 26
Starting A Family 29
Motherhood 33
Take It Like A Man 37
The Sins of The Father 43
Sexually Violated 47
A Life Filled With Shame 53
A Struggle With My Faith 58
My Lost Love 61
A Trial Run 64
I Have Found Jesus! 69
After The Reconciliation 73
The Last Straw 77
Freedom From Fear? 81
My Second Chance for Happiness 84

Where Is The Justice?	91
My Life Falls Apart	96
Traded In For a Motorcycle	99
The Effects of a Broken Heart	105
Three Times Should Be a Charm	108
A Life Change	115
A Church of My Own	120
Another Church - Another Chance	127
Is This As Low As It Gets?	131
Calling It Quits	136
Loss of Identity	140
Grieving Loss of Family	143
Lonely	147
Wanted: Somewhere To Belong	151
Facing Shame Head-On	156
Winter Sunlight	160
Forgiveness	165
Wanting the Best for My Sons	169
The Joy of Grandchildren	172
Freedom and Voice	178
What Is God's Will for Us?	181
Committed To The Journey	188
Recommended Reading	195

Where Are You, God?

Supper was at 5 p.m. without fail and as the dutiful wife, every night I cooked meat, potatoes, and vegetable. Tonight, however, for a change, it was goulash. I filled my husband's plate with food and served him, as always, as he sat at the family dinner table. With a ravishing appetite, he put a heaping forkful of the goulash into his mouth.

"Damn it, this stuff is as hot as hell," he screamed. He spit it out, picked up his plate and threw it against the wall toward the other side of the table where I was sitting.

"Why did you serve me food that was too hot?" he said.

I don't know why I can't get it right, I thought.

"I'm sorry," I said, chopping the food on the tray of my toddler's high chair. I didn't look up, hoping the issue would just pass over; and the food would become cool enough for my husband to eat.

He was a big, strong man well over 6 feet and much, much over 200 pounds. I was five feet four, 110 pounds. Raging, he picked up his corner of the solid wood dining room table, and overturned it as if made of cardboard.

This kind of angry outburst happened on a regular basis; but I was always fearful of what would happen next. My husband had a very short fuse and anything could set him off. When it did, he would throw what he could get his hands on. Whatever was at an arm's length, he would throw at me: a hammer that narrowly missed my head; a screwdriver that imbedded itself in the wood door behind me; a cross saw that took a sliver out of the linoleum

Shame Shame Go Away!

floor; and lit cigarettes that left burns on my face. Scared to death, I never knew what would be hurled in my direction.

This pattern of behavior showed me early in our marriage he was to be feared. It was his way of demonstrating his control over me and I was terrified of him.

As he overturned the table with Samson-like strength, everything spilled to the floor, and the massive wooden leg that had been screwed to the tabletop cracked off.

My two-year old son was screaming as I jumped up, removed him from his chair, and held him close to my breast. He was easily frightened as the yelling and cursing happened often.

I turned to run and get my son out of harm's way, but he reached me before I got to the outside door. He threw me against the wall where the goulash, applesauce and salad were sliding down the wallpaper. I cradled my pregnant belly with the body of my toddler, trying to protect our second son still in my womb.

"God in heaven help me. God, please stop him," I prayed as my head hit the kitchen wall.

"Whatcha say?" he said. Deciding not to repeat it and risk another bump on my head, I didn't respond. He pushed my head against the wall again. "When I ask you something – you answer me, you hear me bitch."

"God, help me," I repeated, shaking like a leaf.

"God doesn't care what happens to you. You're as low as a snake's ass to the ground."

And I believed what he said.

"You can't do anything right."

I believed him.

"Can't you keep your kid quiet? I told you - you're worthless."

Where Are You, God?

I believed him.

I always believed him because what he said was how it was – no questions asked. The names he called me, I was. Where he told me to go, I went. What he told me to do, no matter how horrific, I did. The church had taught me my role was to be a submissive wife.

The night before, as I had walked in the driveway, he steered his car towards me, and I had to jump out of its path. Even one of his beer-drinking buddies who witnessed it shook his head.

I never knew what would happen next so I had to be vigilant when he was on one of his rampages to keep my sons and myself safe. He wanted to keep me, in his words, "barefoot and pregnant."

Yet every Sunday morning, our perfect family, father, mother, and two sons, left our perfect home in our perfect car to attend our perfect church – a church who taught wives to be submissive to their husbands.

My husband, the batterer, marched our family into the church that had been his church from birth.

He wanted everyone to see his attractive wife and adorable children. His extended family was well known in the small Dutch community where he held a prestigious position. He was a proud man. A pious man.

In the congregation sat his parents, grandparents, brothers, sisters, aunts, uncles, cousins, friends, neighbors, and everyone who knew the batterer from birth. They regarded our family as perfect.

No one knew we were victims.

Shame Shame Go Away!

We had all the external markings of a beautiful life. For such a young man he had done well financially. We had a lovely home, a swimming pool, a boat, and a camper. Possessions were very important to him.

For me I just wanted a loving home, free of anger, cursing, and fear.

My life was a nightmare of survival. My sons and I lived it every day and no one could save us.

Was this God's will for us?

Did my family deserve this kind of treatment?

Why, God why?

The Perfect Middle Child

What went wrong? How did my life become so violent?

As the middle daughter of three, my two sisters resembled my father with beautiful dark eyes and olive skin. I took after my mother and had a milky white complexion and acne in my preteen years. My mother told me it was fortunate to resemble Dad's family and I felt as if I didn't belong in this family, or anywhere.

My need for encouragement equaled my need to be shown love. Even at an early age, I was always fearful I would disappoint and even in simple tasks, I lacked confidence to accomplish success. As a good obedient daughter, I did whatever it took to make others happy, especially my mom and dad.

At the age of seven, as I hurried home from school, I crossed the street on an angle instead of staying in the crosswalk. A police officer drove his cruiser down the street, and stopped, rolling down his window.

"Young lady, where do you live?" he asked.

I pointed down the street.

"Do you always cross the street right here?"

I shrugged my shoulders, but didn't say a word.

"You know I could give you a ticket for jaywalking. You didn't use the crosswalk."

Tears filled my eyes as I tried to remain calm, until I started sobbing.

"I'll let you go this time, but don't do it again, okay?"

Shame Shame Go Away!

Nodding my head, I continued to sob as I walked home. Oh no, oh no. I could have gone to jail, I thought. Afraid my mom would find out, I did not tell anyone ever. Keeping this jaywalking secret, I felt like I was a criminal.

The atmosphere in my family's home was tense. There weren't hugs, kisses, or the words, "I love you" between my parents or towards my sisters and me.

In my 30's, I hugged my mother good-bye and tried to give her a kiss on her cheek. She backed away with disgust. This was an ah-ha moment for me, as this was how it had always been.

In elementary school, my Mom would bring me the first day. I was always insecure and afraid of first-time experiences. Mom would say to my new teacher, "She's a little slow, but she'll get it. It will just take her a little longer."

This played into my concern that there was something not quite right with me. In my adult life, I was diagnosed and medicated for Attention Deficit Disorder.

While in elementary school, large families of six to eight children, immigrants from the Netherlands, came to the United States. The children from these families were placed in the Christian school I attended even though they knew nothing of the English language. Besides the language barrier, they were isolated from the other kids because they 'looked different' and owned only one or two dresses. I felt sad for the new Dutch students, and tried to befriend them.

They seemed to be warm, loving and committed toward one another. During recess, they were so happy to see each other. I wanted to be one of them.

The Perfect Middle Child

My grandparents were born in the Netherlands, but my parents were born in the United States. I was accustomed to hearing about the old country, and decided I wanted to be Dutch.

"I want to be a little Dutch girl. Can I, mom, can I?" I said to my mother one day. As normal, my mother ignored me and kept ironing.

I was persistent.

"Why can't I be a little Dutch girl? I want a different name, like Hendricka or Derk."

"I think I want my new name to be Anika. Okay, mom, okay?"

First mom shrugged her shoulders and then gave a nod.

"I want to be called Anika, the good little Dutch girl."

When my mom used my name, she called, "Annie!"

And my response would be "Not Annie, Anika. Anika, the good little Dutch girl."

For around a year, I reminded my mom to call me Anika. My sisters were five years older and younger, respectively, and paid no attention to my request for a name change.

Sensing my family was different than my girlfriends' families, I never asked them to my house to play, for dinner, or for a sleepover. I ate, played and slept at their homes, but never at my house. Our family had secrets we never shared with others.

Every night before mom returned home from work my dad made supper and would drink glass after glass of whiskey while cooking. When mom returned home, she had several glasses of whiskey and coke. Then after supper, dad passed out in his chair. My mom went cold turkey one day and never drank again, but my

Shame Shame Go Away!

father drank until the day he died at age 60. Although I did not recognize it until he passed away, my father was an alcoholic.

My mother worried about unusual and unlikely life circumstances. She was emotionally unstable and a nervous wreck most of the time. My dad often threatened to take her to Cutlerville. Even at a young age, I knew Cutlerville meant the 'nut house' where people went when they lost their mind.

I often found my mother crying, for no particular reason and I couldn't think of why she would be crying.

"Why is Mommy so sad?" I once asked my dad.

After a moment, he said, "Remember mom told you about your baby sister who died soon after she was born. Well, when she thinks about her, she becomes sad."

Later I understood the real reason why she cried so often and it had nothing to do with my dad's excuse

Between the ages of 10 and 18, my dad would ask me to go with him to various sporting activities like the "Golden Gloves" (yearly boxing tournaments) and billiard tournaments. I was not an athlete or interested in watching ball games or competition, but I was honored, because he never asked my sisters, just me. In my eyes, this made me special. My dad never had a son, so I convinced myself I was a substitute son for him.

After the first time we went out together, he pulled into the alley off from the main street, without saying a word. When he opened his door, I started to open mine, not understanding why we were here.

"Just wait here. It'll just be a few minutes," he said. "Lock your door."

The Perfect Middle Child

I did as he said and locking his door, he strolled into the back door of the bar.

As I sat in the car behind the bar in a dark alley, I was terrified. It was an area of homeless drunks and I worried who might be lurking around another vehicle or doorway. I slouched down in the seat and would peek up, looking this way or that way. My heart was pounding so loud I hoped the sound wouldn't penetrate outside of the car. I was worried it might attract those people walking the streets, and someone would try to break into the car. I placed my thumb in my mouth even though as a baby, I never was a thumb-sucker.

I did not dare step outside the car and into the bar to find dad, not only because it would be unsafe, but it would make him very unhappy with me. After an hour or so, he came out.

"Promise me that you won't ever tell Mom what we have done," he said.

In future night-outs, I went with him, even knowing the evening would end up in the bar alley. It wasn't because I had such a wonderful experience, but I could not say, "No, I don't want to go." On our way home each time, dad said, "Don't tell mom what we did." I never told mom or anyone.

Arguments between mom and dad were regular occurrences. When he wanted to go out at night, she flew off the handle. After he died, mom told me about his infidelities and her crying binges made sense to me.

Looking back, I know our nights out together were not used to build our relationship, but rather to meet dad's needs. He used me so he could get out of the house at night and meet his women friends at the bar. It was never because he enjoyed my company.

Shame Shame Go Away!

Other childhood events that remain vivid in my memory were coming home and finding dad applying ice to mom's bloody nose; and dad calling from the bar and telling mom he was going to jump off the city bridge into the river. Both times I was given the 'don't ask' look, and I never did.

Mom and dad never attended any of my school programs, awards or recognition events. No excuse was given as to why neither could attend and I never acted disappointed, but I would make up lies when my friends asked, "Where are your mom and dad?"

In the fifth grade, I participated in 4-H and made an apron and had to model it in competitions which led to the state finals. My parents were busy that night, so I had to get a ride with my friend and her mother to the competition. I beat hundreds of other first year 4-H contenders and won the first place medal.

When I returned home, my mom said, "Well, how was it?"

"You should have seen it," I said. "This is a great big place with lots and lots of people. And when they called my name because I won, I had to walk down from the balcony." I was at a loss for words. "I was so scared, and they gave me this." I tossed the medal into her lap. "Guess I will go up to bed now."

As a 10 year-old, I could not find the words to describe walking across the stage to receive a once in a lifetime award and not share the moment with anyone. As I fell asleep that night, my pillow was wet with tears.

In high school, leading the band as the head majorette was a very important part of my life. My dad attended the high school football games and hoped I made him proud. And with my good grades the band director worked hard to get me a scholarship.

The Perfect Middle Child

Just before my graduation, recognition was given to me at a Band Award Banquet for recipients and their parents. Once again my parents were not able to attend with no reason as to why. As I walked home following the banquet, I again felt very alone.

My younger sister was in the middle school band at that time. She attended the banquet with some friends, and made it home before I did. As I walked into the house, she said to my mom (since dad had already passed out), "Annie won an award. You should have been there." She always had a way of telling it like it was. My mother said nothing.

I turned down the scholarship due to lack of finances and interest from my parents.

"We don't do college in our family, especially for girls," my mom said. "They just get married and have babies anyway."

Neither of my parents attended my graduation from high school, and there was no recognition with an open house or family dinner to commemorate the graduation. My mom gave me money before I left for the commencement.

"Here take Andrew out after graduation for something nice to eat," she said.

After graduation, Andrew (my boyfriend) and I hit the drive thru at the local Kum-Bak Hamburg restaurant. We ate and then he dropped me back off at home.

"I stepped inside the doorway just when you walked across the stage to get your diploma," my mom said as I walked in the house. My heart told me she was not there.

Anika, the little Dutch girl, had survived her childhood without scars, or had she?

The Little Dutch Girl Loved Church

From an early age, I can remember always wanting to be in church. It was home to me.

On Sunday mornings, I would say to my mom, "Are we going to church today?" Either she would make an excuse of why we weren't going or just agree to take me. Often times she and I attended church alone. My dad would still be sleeping, and my two sisters either said they did not feel good or just begged off going with us.

"I think I will just drop you off at the church, and you can live there," my mom often said. Or "You should marry a minister someday, and then you'll get your fill of church."

But it was more than just being in the church for me. Anytime I was there, I felt special. After the worship service, there was Sunday school where I loved to listen to stories from the Bible. It was there my faith was shaped and molded to believe that God loved ME.

My mom would leave after the service so she would have to drive back to pick me up after Sunday school. As soon as we arrived home, with my Bible story papers in hand, I would run upstairs to my bedroom where my dolls awaited me. I would arrange my 'children' on my bed. Then using the papers given me in Sunday school, I would teach my pretend family the lesson from my class.

"Who in the heck is she talking to up there?" my dad would ask my mom.

The Little Dutch Girl Loved Church

"Pay no attention. She's just preaching to her dolls," my mom said.

God had a special purpose for my life even then, although it was beyond my ability to comprehend at that time.

On Sunday afternoons, I begged to go with my Grandma to the Dutch service at the church. Although I couldn't understand a word that was spoken or the hymns they sang, I loved the feeling of being back there again.

On the Sundays mom and I didn't go to church, she would drop me off at the church building just before the service was over. I would hide in the church bathroom until the service was over, and then appear for the Sunday school class. I never wanted my friends to know I had not been in church as they had been with their families.

Two of my girlfriends went to the same church as I did; but their parents were different than mine. Their parents attended church service every Sunday morning and every Sunday evening.

Even back then, I felt guilty. I was trying to hide the fact that my parents drank and fought every day.

From the third grade through the 12th grade, every Wednesday after school, I attended catechism classes. It was the church's requirement that children and teenagers attend these classes. It was there that I learned the foundation of the beliefs in the Dutch church tradition.

Memorization was a huge part of the learning. Answers to eight to ten questions were to be memorized every week. Then in class, the Reverend would drill the students on the questions for that week's lesson.

Shame Shame Go Away!

It was easy for me to memorize, and to be approved by the Reverend was to be approved by God. So I studied hard. Lacking confidence, my voice would crack and shake when it was my turn to speak. Sometimes my voice was so quiet, the Reverend would say, "Could you repeat your answer please?" I wasn't confident that my answer would be the right one, so I would whisper.

With ease, I also memorized the chapters of scripture required each year at my parochial school. Over and over again the night before I needed to recite them in front of the teacher and my classmates, I would practice until they were perfect. I always tried to do my best to get approval from my parents and teachers.

All through high school, I was a spiritually focused teenager. As I approached high school graduation, I was ready to join the church membership. To do so, I needed to appear before the leaders and profess my beliefs as a Christian. I had to wait a month for the meeting and, although I knew what I believed, I felt shaky inside.

This waiting gave me plenty of time to memorize the answers to the 129 questions contained in the Heidelberg Catechism. So any question they presented to me from the catechism, I had the precise answer.

I would go back and forth in my mind as to whether I would be accepted or would be turned down for full membership in the church. My family was not as righteous as my friends' families so in the eyes of the church leaders, I worried whether they thought I would be good enough.

Finally the anticipated night arrived. I sat at a long, polished wooden table with the minister and 12 men who interrogated me on my faith based on the questions from the catechism. One

The Little Dutch Girl Loved Church

question after another, I answered each one perfectly. At the end, I was asked to step outside the room. The door didn't latch all the way, so with my ear pressed against the wall near the door, I listened.

"So what do you think," said the Reverend. "Do you think her answers were sincere enough?

I held my breath, wondering what sincerity had to do with memorizing the catechism questions. A vote was taken, and the Reverend came out in the hall.

"We offered prayer before our decision, and we feel it is God's will that we accept you into full membership of the church. Your public profession of faith will be a week from Sunday," he said.

Whew! What a relief. I was accepted. I knew I was a child of God long before I appeared before the presence of the leaders of the church. God had accepted me, and now the 12 male elders and deacons had agreed with God.

It was an honor to profess my faith before the church. Now that I was 18 and had a driver's license, I didn't have to ask, "Mom, the church has a potluck. Can you bring me?" or "Wednesday night is choir practice, mom, can you bring me?"

I was relieved I wasn't dependent upon my mother to bring me to the many church events I wanted to attend. Most of all, I loved feeling that I belonged somewhere. I was part of the family of God.

So how could this good little Dutch girl be begging God for protection just six years later?

Falling In Love

During a basketball game in the first few months of high school, I fell in love. It was my first date, and we had taken the school bus to an away game. Lee was sitting next to me when he reached over and took my hand. My heart was beating so fast – thump, thump, thump. Was it going to pop out of my chest? My head was spinning. Am I going to pass out? This guy really likes ME!

On the way home we held hands, and when we arrived back at the school, he walked me home.

"Can we go out together again?" he asked at my door.

I was thinking yes, yes, yes, but with a calm voice, I said, "Sure."

He ducked his 6'3"frame down and kissed me. I felt the blood rush through my veins. I was in love.

For the next year and a half, we were a couple. At school, after school at his house, or walking back home from school, we could not keep our hands off each other. We exchanged class rings to make sure everyone knew we were taken. Certainly this was love.

He was older than me, had a driver's license and soon a car. We shared the same locker. Walking down the hall between classes, we slipped each other love notes. Excitement heightened as I read that hour's note. Answering every note took priority instead of participating in class. We wore our 'going steady' shirts and sweaters with pride. Our lives were intertwined in every aspect of our lives.

Then, after 18 months, it felt different. Missing was that indescribable magnet when we looked at each other. I could not put into words this change between us. It was as if he and I were worlds apart. Feeling insecure, I panicked. Wait a minute, what's happening? Did I do something wrong? What did I say? I asked myself over and over, what did I do?

"What's wrong?" I asked him.

He did not give me an answer. I needed him to love me. I would do whatever I could to make him love me.

I was saving every penny to buy contact lens at that time and had an opportunity to make big bucks babysitting New Year's Eve.

"Honey, you want to come over after the kids go to bed? I'll be there late, real late," I said. He gave no response.

Needing to just hear his voice for affirmation, I called him later that New Years Eve.

"He's not home," his mother said. "He went to a New Year's Eve party at Cheryl's house."

Cheryl, who is Cheryl? I didn't know any Cheryl.

I froze as I opened my locker the day after holiday vacation and tears filled my eyes. The pictures of us we hung on the locker door together were gone. I looked around. Was he watching me? When did he do this? No warning. No argument. Not even a discussion. Then the tears turned to anger. What did I do to deserve this?

In a daze, I walked down the hall, and saw him talking to classmates. My heart skipped a beat for a moment or two as I stopped in my tracks. This must be what a heart attack felt like. Was this the same heart I thought would pop out of my chest when he first took my hand more than a year earlier?

"Now who are you going to date?" my mom asked when I told her about the break-up. "What will others think since he broke up with you? He was such a nice guy. Thought for sure you would marry him."

She never wanted her daughters without boyfriends as she was afraid it would be a reflection on her if one of her daughters was unmarried.

"I'm hardly an old maid, Mom. I'm just 16 years old." Would I find someone to date?

Lord, For My Mother, Give Me Someone to Date

Two weeks after the break-up I met the guy I would marry. I vowed that no matter what, no one would break up with me again. I would do whatever it took to keep him.

Although we lived in different towns and attended different schools, we quickly became a couple. Andrew had not dated before, and was not a gentleman like my first love, who had treated me like a princess. Andrew didn't wait for me when we were walking in or out of somewhere or hold the door. There were no overt acts of caring, kindness or affection. Yet, it never occurred to me that this was not how I wanted to be treated. I accepted it, and just thought it came along with the territory of having a boyfriend.

I did learn to watch out if life didn't go his way. He shouted threats or exhibited irrational behavior. On a date one night, he was in one of his moods, angry one moment and giving me the silent treatment the next. When he dropped me off at my house, my brother-in-law's Volkswagen was parked in my driveway. When my brother-in-law left the house later, he found his car gone. Looking down the street, he found his vehicle parked in the neighbor's front yard. Andrew was parked watching until the car was found. He had pushed the small car out of my driveway on to my neighbor's lawn. Did it occur to him what my family would think of him? As his girlfriend, I was ashamed of Andrew's behavior, but I never told him so.

Shame Shame Go Away!

Sometimes he violated the law by being destructive to the property of others. I believed he was just immature and showing off to impress me. He was mean, sometimes vicious. If an animal crossed the road, instead of veering away from the animal, he would chase it so he could kill it. Even though it bothered me, I never said anything. I just worked hard to make sure I knew what his 'way' was so I could do everything that way. I did not believe I had a voice to express my way.

"Can you believe it? Anne's 17, and doesn't have a license. Afraid to take the road test," he teased me in front of our friends. "Whatcha scared of? The policeman?"

I felt ashamed that night since I was the only one in our group who didn't have a driver's license.

"I want to get my license," I said to my mom, as I came into the house after my date. "Either you or dad need to take me practice driving so I can pass my road test."

"Let your dad take you," my mom said. "It makes me too nervous."

Looking at my dad, passed out in his chair, I wondered how I would convince him that this was important to me. I did, and several weeks later, I proudly presented my license to Andrew. He wasn't impressed.

The first time I met Andrew's family was not the best timing, as we returned to his house after an accident we had with his family's car.

"It wasn't my fault. A corvette came over the center line and hit me head on," Andrew explained. This was not met with an ounce of understanding in the hostile family environment.

Lord, For My Mother, Give Me Someone to Date

"You're paying for it out of your money" yelled his parents, both of them chiding him for his stupidity.

"I know. I plan to pay for the repairs," Andrew said. "The guy has insurance but I plan to pay for it."

No recognition was given by his folks that I was even there. There was no introduction and not a word was said to me. No one even asked if anyone was hurt. There was just anger that Andrew had cracked up the car.

I figured the next time he took me to his house, formal introductions would occur, and the overall atmosphere would be much better. It wasn't.

We sat in the living room waiting to be called for dinner.

"Hurry up, sit down, it's getting cold," his mother said in an angry tone. Sitting at the dinner table with the family, the kids were not only quiet but they had sullen faces. Their mother's angry persona dominated the room.

With a soft, apologetic voice, Andrew's father said the Lord's Prayer. It was the family's ritual as they were a religious farm family. No one initiated table conversation. I looked at the plaque hanging above the table, HOME SWEET HOME. I doubted that any member of this family thought the farmhouse was Home Sweet Home. When the meal was over, his father asked if there was dessert. This initiated another round of raging one-sided conversation. The meal was concluded when Andrew's father read a chapter of the Bible. I don't believe a soul there heard a word he said.

"Sorry, Ma's been a little mad lately," Andrew apologized to me after dinner. "Well, actually a lot. She's either yelling at us or won't speak to us, sometimes for weeks."

"She doesn't talk to any of you for weeks?" I asked. "How about your dad?"

"He's scared to death of her. She's angry at him all the time. Never a kind word, she hates him. I told him more than once he should divorce her."

"What did he say about that?"

"My dad said divorce is a sin. The church is against divorce."

After my first meal with Andrew's family, I thought it was sad the family was held hostage by the power and control of the wife and mother. It was apparent to me that not one of them believed it would get better.

Andrew's maternal grandparents lived in a nearby community. It was known to family and neighbors that Grandpa had a temper and treated sweet little Grandma with abuse and disrespect for 64 years. He verbally insulted her by demanding she jump to his every whim. 'Woman, get me this or get me that.' No one dared stand in Pa's way.

Andrew's mother exhibited the same kind of abuse and control over her family as her father had done with his wife and family. Just like her dad, everyone was too scared to challenge her behavior.

I once heard that boys who are abused grow up to abuse others. In this case, it was the daughter (Andrew's mother) who grew up in an abusive household and her childhood rage made victims of her husband and children. Since there were no negative consequences to her dad's behavior, why would her life be any different?

I continued to date Andrew throughout high school, graduation, and our first jobs. The Christmas following graduation, he gave me a diamond, and asked me to marry him. Of course, I said, "Yes." I didn't know how to say 'No' to a man. And I was convinced I could change him to show me love.

But the image of Andrew's dear sweet Grandma who lived with her tyrant husband for 64 years was etched into my memory.

Oh God, please don't let this be me.

The Chapel Wedding

It was early spring and thunderstorms and heavy rains dominated our wedding day.

It was tradition in my family to marry young and I was the oldest member to walk down the chapel aisle at age 19.

"I don't want to be married on Friday the 13th. It would be bad luck for our marriage," I told Andrew. To insure good luck, we were married on Thursday, the 12th.

Taking a bath hours before my wedding, a current of electricity raced through my body, and I jumped out of the tub. A lightning bolt had hit the faucet.

I should have paid attention as this one bolt of lightning was just a sample of the many storms ahead in my marriage's future.

"Sorry, I can't make it. I think I have the flu," Andrew said to me in a telephone call just before I left for the chapel.

"Oh, no, how sick are you?" I said. Believing him, I was concerned for his well-being. Even though not showing up for his wedding would have been his problem, I thought I needed to solve it for him.

"Just kidding," he said. He was making a joke; however, it was a cruel one for a nervous bride.

My wedding was beautiful, just how I had imagined it to be. As inexperienced as we were at what true love looked like, we thought this must be it.

"I want a nice reception for my Annie," my dad said. "And especially a gorgeous wedding cake." My father worked in a

The Chapel Wedding

bakery and knew the best in the cake-making business. It was decorated in my favorite flower, pink roses. It was as gorgeous as my dad wanted it to be. My parents were of meager means but had borrowed money for a full dinner for our 125 guests.

"She's been the very best daughter any father could have," my father told Andrew as the reception was coming to an end. "I never had to spank her or discipline her. She never needed it. She has such a soft heart, so be gentle with her." Andrew assured my dad he would be good to me.

Dutch tradition is to chivalry a couple following their marriage. This meant after the wedding reception friends would chase them. The purpose was to instill fear that they would be separated on the first night they could legally spend together. Dumb? Yes!

Motioning with her hand, my mom told us the time had come to leave so those who were planning to follow would never know we had left. Thinking back, as I looked into my mom's eyes, I think she was trying to tell me that my life would never be the same.

A mother's intuition knows when her child is in danger.

Will You Please Forgive Me?

Neither Andrew nor I knew what a happy Christian home looked like, but we were hopeful we could make one. With excitement, we rented a small apartment and purchased furniture. Both of us had minimal paying jobs, but financially our combined income would pay our bills.

I had the vision of happy times of cooking, cleaning, and making a nice home where our love would grow.

While I remembered reading in Proverbs 5:18: Rejoice in the wife of your youth, Andrew did no rejoicing in me. I could do nothing to please him. He found fault with everything I tried to do. I had very little experience cooking or doing laundry, so I lacked confidence. He found fault with what I wore, how I acted, even my name irritated him, "Anne . . . what a stupid name," he said. I had no control over the name I was given. It was just a plain name. How stupid could it be?

"I'm sorry. Whatever I did, I'm sorry. Please forgive me." Over and over again I would tell him I was sorry. He would go days without speaking a word to me, never telling me what I had done wrong. His silence initiated the pattern of my trying to please him, no matter what it took. My life became filled with the fear of the unknown. Trying to make him happy became my total focus.

Our intimacy was anything but sweet expressions of love. I wanted to please him so I went along with everything he suggested.

Will You Please Forgive Me?

We met some people at the races and he invited them over so we could play spin the bottle. As the bottle spun, whoever it landed on had to remove an article of clothing. I had never heard of such a game. Later he used that same bottle on me in a sexual way. I never felt confident enough to say, "Don't do that to me. I don't like it. It scares me."

Within the first year of our marriage, he wanted me to invite my teenage sister over to our apartment so he could have sex with her at the same time we were making love. I lived with the fear that he would sexually assault her so I protected her by making sure she was never alone with him.

Yelling – swearing – throwing things – kicking – punching the wall. He threatened me with his anger. He scared me with verbal, emotional and psychological abuse. I became a bundle of nerves.

Some mornings I called in sick to my job after he went to work. I had made him mad again and needed him to love me. Whatever had made him mad, I would make it up to him. So I would walk to the meat market and buy a special cut of meat. Back at our small apartment I would prepare a wonderful dinner. But no matter what I tried to do, he was never happy. His short fuse made me shake with the unknown and my fear of Andrew never subsided.

After our first year of marriage, before we were 21 years old and with my father- in-law's help, we bought our first home. We were so excited and I felt like we were on the track to the good life.

Andrew was very ambitious and was willing to take on any home project. But whatever he was doing, when things did not go as planned, I ran because his frustration turned into anger, and his anger meant he would throw, kick, or tear whatever he could get his hands on. It became unbearable for me to be around him while he worked on anything in the house, yard, or car. He complained because I didn't show interest in what he was doing, but the truth was that I just didn't want to be hit. Running before the violence began was one of many ways I sought to survive.

It was expected in the community where we lived that after a couple had their own home, they would start a family. Unfortunately, evaluating if the marriage fostered a stable home was not a necessity before bringing a baby into such dysfunction.

Starting a Family

Soon our focus was on the expectation of the arrival of our first child. With diligence, he created a wooden cradle for our bundle of joy. We painted the room and bought baby furniture. There were moments when I thought I had a perfect home and a perfect life. I had a husband who went to church with me and we were having our first baby. Then something would happen that would make me realize my life was not how it appeared.

When I was seven months pregnant, I resigned from my receptionist position to prepare for the birth of our baby and my office was giving me a farewell luncheon. I was dressed in my Sunday best maternity dress prepared to go to the luncheon when something I said upset Andrew. Standing in the back entrance to our home, he grabbed me by my necklace and choked me. I gasped for air until the necklace broke, spilling beads on to the floor. I took a deep breath of air, relieved that the violent episode was over.

Later that night, while we lay in bed, he put the pillow over my head. After fighting him, he released the pillow, laughing. "It was just a joke," he said. I was not humored. After I knew he was sleeping, I felt the urgency to seek safety so I quietly got out of bed. I didn't dare take our only car so I would need to walk from our rural home. But where would I go? I thought of his old maid aunt. She really liked me so perhaps she would take me in. I was scared. Was I being ridiculous or could I be in danger since there were two harmful incidences in the same day? What would happen next?

I looked out the door of our rural home. It was 18 miles from any of my family and at least 10 miles from his aunt. It was snowing and blowing, and the wind chill was below zero. I envisioned walking in knee deep snow, and decided I would never make it alive. Defeated I climbed back into bed next to my abuser.

When morning came, I tried to talk to him about his actions from the day before.

"You know I have an anger problem. Get used to it," he said. "Just don't do things to piss me off. If you don't like it, don't let the door hit you in the ass when you leave." I did not try to talk to him about his behavior again.

I wrote him letters expressing the deepest aches of my heart; how much I loved him; how I wanted to be a good wife; and how I wanted to be given a chance to become the wife he wanted. But I would never give him these letters, afraid of upsetting him, and being assaulted. I wanted to tell him how scared I was of his behavior, yet I always stopped myself before I took that risk.

In a couple months the baby would come; and I believed we would be a family. He would be so happy with the baby and that would make him happy with me too or so I thought. I believed he would start to change once he became a father.

I thought it was my responsibility to change him or as he said, get used to his anger. It was either do not make him mad or just live with it. Those were my options.

Starting A Family

The baby was weeks over due and Andrew was impatient. He made me run up and down the basement steps, trying to start my labor. He became disgusted because nothing helped.

Finally the doctor hospitalized me and started my labor. The process was long and hard. Andrew became angry with me because he could not figure out why all the other women in adjoining labor rooms were delivering their babies, and my labor was so slow.

"Just have it," he said. "You're embarrassing me. Why are you are taking so long? Just have it, will ya?"

I felt like I had failed. Why couldn't I do it like the other mothers in labor? The pain was so intense, hour after hour after hour. Perhaps it was as he said, I couldn't do anything right. As usual, I felt I was not good enough.

Instead of staying with me while in labor, he went home. After all, he needed his sleep. While he was gone, I asked the doctor if he could do something to speed it up because my husband was becoming impatient. After a while, the doctor broke my water, and our precious son was born 12 hours later.

The following morning as I laid in the maternity ward recovering from a lengthy delivery process, my doctor walked in with our son.

"Your son has developed a birthmark on his head," he said. He handed him over to me and exited the room.

I took the bundle into my arms and pulled back the baby's blanket. Shocked at what I saw, I pulled the blanket back further and further. On my baby's blond head was a deep purple birthmark that appeared to cover half of his head, neck and down onto his shoulder. I panicked. How would my husband accept our baby with this mark? I felt like I needed to escape.

I laid Baby Mark down on my hospital bed and as I struggled to get into the room's bathroom, with my IV hooked up to my arm, my eyes filled with tears. Andrew would blame me. He would say I took too long to deliver. He would think it was my fault for the birthmark on our son's head even though the doctor had said it was there from the moment of conception.

After a good cry and the realization that I could not escape through the bathroom's window, I returned to my bed. As I peeked at my precious son, I was ashamed I had even considered running. I would not abandon him and I would never allow Andrew to do to him what he had done to me.

Little did I know I would end up breaking my promise to baby Mark.

Motherhood

Would I ever have time to put on my makeup again? None of the baby books told me that having a baby takes 24/7 and changes your life forever. Sterilizing bottles, making formula, bathing, feeding and nurturing baby, changing diapers, and lots of laundry, including bleaching cloth diapers were part of the responsibilities of adjusting to life with a baby.

Mark was born without the innate ability to suck. In the hospital, I learned how to teach him to drink. Feeding him four ounces took an hour and a half. Two hours later the routine started all over again. It took my entire day and evening to get everything done. Afraid of failing, I was a nervous mother who was serious about the demands of motherhood.

Sensing my anxiety, Mark suffered from colic. He would cry for hours and nothing would comfort him.

"Shut that kid up, will ya?" his dad would say.

Mark's crying always started around 4 pm and continued until he fell asleep exhausted around 9 pm. Andrew returned home from work, and expected dinner to be ready at 5 pm. With the baby crying through dinner, a peaceful eating experience was an illusion. I kept thinking that I was sorry our baby wouldn't stop crying and that I didn't like it either. But I didn't dare say this because I did not want Andrew to explode. My anxiety over the supper scene every night created more colic for Mark. It was a vicious cycle and I believed it was my responsibility to control.

Shame Shame Go Away!

Following supper and in a disgusted mood, Andrew would go out to his garage workshop and drink beer until midnight with his friends.

After getting the baby asleep at night, I would take a church hymnal and sing to calm my nerves. Each night was the same until bedtime, when my husband would come in after consuming too many beers.

Andrew took very little interest in the care of our child. He did not hold him, feed him, or change him. I soon determined our son was an inconvenience for Andrew.

I was very aware of Mark's birthmark and worried that it was my fault. Perhaps my difficult delivery had caused the mark. Or maybe the sex we had during my pregnancy was too rough, and it made the mark. At his first month's checkup, the pediatrician said it was called a port wine stain and there was nothing I could have done to prevent it from happening. On Mark's tiny blond head, it was very noticeable and even though there was no reason to be ashamed of the mark, I dressed him in a different hat with every outfit.

Although Mark's frame was small and he grew slowly, he was an exceptionally strong baby – strong willed and strong body. All of his motor skills, sitting, crawling and walking, were ahead of the charts.

I couldn't keep up with him and was often chasing him to insure he would not hurt himself. Hyperactive and inquisitive, he was always on the go, one step ahead of me, destroying everything in his path. Getting into drawers and cupboards, pulling out utensils, cleaning supplies, pots and pans, unrolling the toilet paper or throwing toys into the toilet were everyday occurrences.

Motherhood

Mark loved to climb on the table, cupboard or out of bed. I would try to keep him focused playing with his toys and when needed, would swat him on his butt and tell him, "No, no" but I was rarely able to channel his energy.

Toddler Mark began to fear his dad the day he picked him up and threw him. To Andrew there was never a gentle, controlled approach to misbehavior. He would just hit, throw or kick.

"Gotta let him know who's boss," he would say. While Andrew spent very little time around his son, he expected perfection from him and my control of the toddler's behavior. He would make sure Mark knew who was in control, and that daddy was to be feared. At a very early age, Andrew's loud yelling or abusive discipline initiated fear of his father. Mark learned to protect his head by ducking, cowering, or covering it with his arms. Forty years later, he still ducks with any sudden movement toward him.

I was shocked to see blood trickle down my toddler's lip for the first time, and realized it was unlikely I could protect him as I promised on the day of his birth. Andrew demanded that I not defend our son.

"Don't baby him," he would say. With much regret, I obeyed and did not protect him. I could not stop Andrew's rage without paying the price.

Instead of processing what bringing another child into the world would mean, we decided Mark needed a baby brother. I was oblivious to the fact that two babies would not make us anymore a family than one.

"Are you out of your mind?" my mom said, "Another baby!" Without her permission, I had become pregnant with our second son. After another difficult delivery, beautiful baby Michael was

Shame Shame Go Away!

born. Did I really think my husband would help me anymore with two babies?

Take It Like A Man

Content with our family of two sons, I was proud to be their mother and they became my total focus in life. My goal was to raise them like all the baby books told me was the best. What the baby books did not address was the struggle to keep them safe.

Beginning as toddlers, their father hit them, grabbed them by their hair or arm, picked up their small bodies, and threw them.

One summer day I went with a friend to an early morning sidewalk sale. I hired a babysitter to take care of our sons. My husband worked early morning and returned late morning for lunch. When I returned, he was back at work following his lunch break and something was seriously wrong with eight-month old, Michael. For over 24 hours he would not stop screaming. I took him to the pediatrician who diagnosed him with the first of three broken collar bones Michael would sustain in his pre-school years. The doctor questioned me as to how my baby could have sustained this broken bone. I did not have an answer. How had our eight month old son sustained a broken collar bone? Neither Andrew nor the sitter had an answer.

"Stop it, you hun-yucks," Andrew would yell as the boys played out in the yard. Whenever I heard his loud voice, I would come running to the sliding glass door, and witness one of our sons being kicked or thrown. I would hide behind the draperies, wanting to protect them, but not doing so. Fearing his abuse of me, I froze like an ice sculpture. I did not run out of the house to help them and carried that shame in my heart for not defending my own flesh and blood.

Even animals protect their young from predators – even to their own death. What kind of a mother was I? When he wasn't watching, I would check their bruises. I kissed their ouwies, or gave them a hug, wanting them to know I loved them and cared that they were hurt. What was going on in their tiny hearts and minds?

Looking into their eyes, I saw fear. They didn't have to say a word, but I believed they were begging me to help them. I had so much guilt, so much shame. I had not only failed as a wife, but I failed as a mother. Bad wife and now, bad mother.

"Just leave them in the car," he said "It will go much faster."

We were purchasing supplies for a camping trip and Andrew could purchase what we needed alone. Concerned about the safety of our sons, Mark and Michael were only four and two years old. I wanted to stay with them in the car; but instead I did what he said.

When we came out of K-Mart, we noticed that Mark was out of the car. He had unlocked the door and stepped into an empty parking space. Inquisitive, he had seen a coin on the ground, and wanted to claim it.

Yelling obscenities, Andrew took off running toward our son who had jumped back into the car. As I ran after my husband, my heart was in my throat. This would be bad for Mark. Andrew grabbed the four-year-old by his hair and punched him. Blood rushed out of his nose.

"Take it like a man, cry baby, take it like a man," his father said as Mark sobbed.

Take It Like A Man

A man? Was his father being a man by punching a poor defenseless pre-schooler?

Mark's blood was running down into his mouth. As I reached into the glove compartment to grab a Kleenex, my husband said, "Don't help him."

Looking at my son's tear and blood stained face, I quickly wiped it anyway.

The following day we had plans to leave on vacation to the Upper Peninsula. "The vacation is off. I'm not taking these hunyocks anywhere," Andrew screamed. Pointing at Mark, he said, "He ruined it."

Knowing how we would all suffer at the hands of Andrew if we stayed home, I begged him to change his mind so we could continue with our long planned vacation.

"I promise I will keep them quiet. They'll be good. I'll bring books and read to them, and I will color with them. I will sit with them in the back seat and entertain them. I promise."

My husband agreed with those conditions, and the vacation went on as planned. Still I felt full of tension, because every day – all day – I was a buffer between my pre-schoolers and their father, never knowing whom or what would upset him the next time.

At a nearby campsite we sat by the fire with other adult campers after the kids had been put to bed. Mark always had problems falling asleep and he called out for me.

"I'll take care of him," Andrew said as he stepped inside the camper. The next thing I heard was Mark's whimpering cry. His father had punched him on the side of his head, leaving a big bruise.

Shame Shame Go Away!

"What happened to your face, Mark," grandpa (Andrew's dad) said when we visited them after returning home from the camping trip.

"Oh, he ran into a sharp edge of a counter of the camper," his father said, explaining the huge bruise on the temple of Mark's head.

Mark looked at me and I'm sure he was wondering if I would go along with the lie. I remained silent, reaffirming that whatever my husband said had to be the gospel truth.

Every night if their father was in the house and not in his workshop, our sons were expected to give him a kiss on his cheek before they went to bed. Andrew had never shown them affection, not a hug, a kiss, nor an 'I love you.'

After telling the boys to give their dad a good night kiss, Mark said to me in the kitchen, "Why, Mom, why? Why do I have to kiss him? He isn't nice."

I knew Mark was right, but if the kiss was ignored, all of us would have to pay.

"Because even if he isn't nice to us, God wants us to be nice to him," I answered in what I thought was the correct reply of a Christian mother.

"I don't like God very much," my son said.

We lived on a rural acre of land, and one afternoon, while Mark was playing near the pool and swing set, he found a litter of wild bunnies. Mark loved animals, big, small, wild or domestic.

"Look dad, newborn bunnies. So soft and cuddly," he said as he picked up one of the bunnies.

"They'll eat the leaves off my cauliflower plants," Andrew said as he grabbed the bunny out of Mark's hand. "Good for nothing." His size 12 cowboy boots stomped on every one of the bunnies.

Did Mark identify with those bunnies? Was it no wonder Mark was scared to death of his father? Anytime his father just lifted his hand for any reason, Mark cowered with his hands over his head, as that was where his father hit him. I cringed with the thought of what this was doing to his brain.

There was a young man in our community named Stuie. He was a loner, never pursuing a job, and just wandering the streets with his belongings in his backpack.

"You'll never amount to anything. You'll just be a bum, like Stuie," Andrew said to nine-year-old Mark. Did Andrew really think his son would be nothing more than a mentally challenged homeless bum?

Michael, from the very beginning of his young abused life, never shed a tear. I believed Michael learned from his brother Mark. When you cry, he hits you harder and longer. Kicked, thrown, or hit, he defied his father with a look. He would squint his eyes and scowl his forehead. It looked like an 'I dare you'. It seemed that he was saying, 'just wait until I grow up and I'm bigger than you, then I'll get even.' Michael stuffed his anger inside, without tears, and despised his father's abuse.

One Friday night, Michael had asked a friend to sleep over. I had given him a small television off the back porch to take to his basement bedroom so they could watch television. When his father arrived home, he noticed the T.V. was not on the porch.

"Where is it?" he yelled.

"Michael has it." Before I could tell him I had given him permission to take it to his room, Andrew flew into a rage. He

Shame Shame Go Away!

ran downstairs, picked up his 10-year-old-son by the front of his shirt, ripping it leaving only the ribbing, and kicked him on his bare back. Without shedding a tear, Michael stared at his father as he left the room. His overnight friend decided he had to leave and walked home, probably wondering if he was the next victim. Michael did not leave his room for the remainder of the night.

Later in the evening, I went downstairs to see what Michael was doing. He was sleeping with the medal he had won at a school competition that day still around his neck. The imprint of his father's foot was on his back, an image burned into my brain. I wondered what image was imprinted on Michael's heart.

Michael had really excelled that day in a school athletic competition. He couldn't wait to show his dad his medal but never had the opportunity.

Dinnertime with youngsters can be a delightful time of sharing the day's events. This was not the case in our kitchen. Spilling milk during a meal was a major catastrophe equal to a tsunami following an earthquake. Degrading the child was a necessity, as well as the clumsy act itself.

If elbows were on the dinner table, Andrew went after their fingers and arms with a fork, often leaving fork teeth marks on broken skin.

Abuse by embarrassment, humiliation, and degradation was an every day event. What was worse for my young sons, the physical or verbal abuse? Or maybe it was the fear of the unknown. My sons were denied to express their feelings, and to be raised in a loving Christian family.

The Sins of the Father

Our family was religious so we had our infant sons baptized as was our church tradition. In a covenant with God, as parents, we promised to instruct our children and to show by example how to live a Christian life.

Is abuse an example of being a Christian?

Were my boys taught the commandment to honor their father and mother, when their hearts were filled with fear over their father's behavior?

Putting the dog out on a chain as we left for church, he broke loose from my grasp and ran into the yard. Andrew grabbed the chain and angrily whipped it across the calves of my legs, bruising my skin as it ripped my nylons.

"Get into the car," he yelled to us, "We're late."

"Wait a minute I need to change my nylons." I said.

"No time, just get into the car."

I obeyed. On the way to church, he was yelling and swearing, verbally and emotionally abusing all three of us.

As our family sat in church, my bruises oozing blood, what message did it send to our sons? Did his Christianity make any sense to them when the fifth commandment was read in church? *Honor your father and your mother. Exodus 20:5.*

Did fulfilling a promise to God mean parading your family to church every Sunday although your children had witnessed their mother being abused only moments before?

Shame, Shame, Go Away!

What Andrew wanted, he got. He had an insatiable need to steal and was convinced he could succeed by not being caught. This was not simply slipping something into his pocket. He stole big items like a riding lawn mower, lumber from a worksite, bushes and shrubs from a nursery, a rotor-tiller from someone's garden, and much more.

I knew he stole many things and some nights he would tell me what or where he was going. As I lay in bed, I worried and wondered if he would be caught, arrested, and sent to jail. I was afraid it would embarrass all of us when the news hit the conservative community where we lived.

Our sons also knew he stole. When they were 6 and 8 years old, they were with him when he stole two snowmobiles on a trailer parked by someone's driveway for sale. They were for sale, not for stealing. Andrew backed up his vehicle, hitched up the trailer, and drove away. The stolen snowmobiles became new toys for the boys.

Andrew's belief was that since their dad stole the snowmobiles for them, the boys, with gratitude, would want to drive them. They had no interest in driving the snowmobiles around the yard every day after school. But with my insistence, they did so until the day they dumped one of them into the ditch. The anxiety waiting for the outcome of Andrew's response was debilitating. Would he just yell obscenities and call them names? Would he throw something at them, or would he physically throw them?

All three of us became fearful whenever something was broken or went wrong while Andrew was at work. At times, we physically shook, became nauseated, or broke down crying hysterically.

Even at a young age, the boys wanted to protect me from their father when they couldn't even protect themselves. My son, Mark, said to me, "I will take care of you, Mom." Michael once said, "Let me protect you, Mama."

When they could not stick up for me when he called me names or threatened me, they felt guilty and worthless.

Andrew demanded that, as boys, they were to be rough and tough. "Be a man," he would tell them. Their father was a poor model of how to be a man who honors his wife and loves his children unconditionally.

No matter how much I loved my sons, supported them, protected them and reinforced their self-worth, his abuse overshadowed that love.

One Sunday, a fear-filled day of rage and abuse, my husband was taking a nap. It was quiet and serene. I decided he should sleep forever. I went to the gun cabinet, and took two of the six guns out. I opened the ammunition drawer and took out several boxes. Removing different bullets and looking at the guns, I realized I did not understand the concept of guns, bullets, and how to load them. With regret, I put them away, but for a few moments I was hopeful I could keep him quiet forever. The thought that I would pay the consequences for my actions was not reality.

Helpless to change my life and hopeless for a way out, I begged God to let me die in my sleep. When morning came, I asked God why my prayer wasn't answered. Please, God, don't make me face another day. Then I would remember that I needed

Shame, Shame, Go Away!

to protect my sons. If I died, my sons would have to face their father alone.
    I could never abandon them! Never!

Sexually Violated

It was inevitable. Since no boundaries were placed on his behavior outside the bedroom, sexual abuse entered early into my marriage. I believed it was my duty to do what my husband wanted and I had no power to stop him. The Bible says I must be subject to my husband. I thought being subject to him was a spiritual necessity to keep his interest. I was desperate for love and if it meant enduring pain, sacrificing my dignity, and feeling shame, I went along with it. I needed my husband to want me and need me, but most of all to love me. But I hated how he violated me.

Since we were each other's first sexual experience, I couldn't understand how all of this horrible sexual deviation began.

Andrew teased me about the conservative clothes I wore and compared me to my young sister.

"Joanne wears low neck blouses that show cleavage. My wife wears turtlenecks," he would say.

I was not comfortable with publically exposing my body since I was insecure about my sexuality. He mocked my sexual inhibitions.

When he first introduced the idea of going to a XXX rated movie, I was mortified.

"What do they do there?" I asked. I was afraid I would have to be naked as well. He explained that it was movies showing people having sex and thought we could learn some new ways.

Shame Shame Go Away!

As we stood in line to get tickets for the show, I looked around and feared someone I knew would see me.

It was at the movies where I was first learned about sex toys. We were married less than two years when my husband bought these items from the dirty bookstore to use them as we made love. It didn't feel good. It hurt. He was mean when he used them and it caused me pain. I was afraid of what his using them would do to my female organs. More than physically, it was degrading to me. He carved some of these sex toys out of wood in his garage workshop and then brought them in as if I would be excited to have these objects pushed into my body. My self-respect died more and more with each experience.

God gave couples the fulfilling way to express deep sacred love through sexual intercourse. Was it God's will to take this beautiful act of love between two committed people and make it evil? The Bible records that God inspired the leaders of Israel to declare sex in this way to be illegal.

The horrible acts resembled torture as he raped me anally and used bestiality for his sexual gratification. The spirit of my soul disintegrated.

Yet I was convinced that I was always to blame for everything so I took the responsibility for whatever he did to me. The more he degraded my body in ways I never knew existed, the more he convinced me I deserved it. Just when I thought I had endured all I could, he would conjure up another idea. I believed I would be cursed and held accountable to God for allowing him access to me in this abusive way.

How could he think this had anything to do with love? Love was patient; lust required immediate satisfaction. Love was kind;

lust was harsh. Love did not demand its own way; lust did not care about the rights of the other. Lust resulted in self-disgust and hate. What he did to me was not love! It wasn't even lust. It was sexual abuse. I never suggested or encouraged any of these acts and I derived no pleasure or benefit from any of this behavior.

How could he think I ever enjoyed these things? Obviously, he didn't care.

"If we found a couple willing, we could switch sex partners," he said one day. "It would be fun, and improve our sex life."

I could not imagine taking my clothes off in front of another man. I was self conscious and lacked confidence about my body and the sex act itself. I could not imagine the idea of having intercourse with someone just for the sake of sex. The idea that I had the right to say no never felt like an option for me. What he said, we did.

I thought that maybe if I just ignored the idea, he would forget it. He did not.

Having sex with my husband meant being demeaned, and I wanted our sex life to be different. I wanted him to show me love by gently making love to me. If I endured this swapping game, maybe he would be more excited by me and it might help our sex life.

Since childhood, I had maintained a relationship with a friend. Our husbands became friends, and as couples, we had a great time together. The idea of switching partners was something my husband brought up with them. My friend also pushed for this rendezvous, but I could tell her husband did not want to participate. He went along with it just as I did.

Shame Shame Go Away!

With our small children, we went on vacation together with the purpose of sleeping with one another's spouse.

The first night as I lay in bed with my friend's husband, we could hear our spouses enjoying each other. He jumped up, sobbing and ran out into the night and disappeared. Andrew and my friend ran after him.

I curled up in a fetal position, embarrassed, ashamed and crying. This was the end of our mate swapping with this couple. Her husband never wanted to see us again.

Later I realized that a relationship had existed between my friend and my husband before the mate-swapping incident and it continued long after this horrific experience.

My best friend had deceived me and now our cherished friendship was over. I experienced loss of personal self-esteem, loss of marital trust, and loss of a dear friendship. A long term friendship between two childhood friends and two couples was terminated. Was it because my husband was bored in bed or because he had lust for another woman? Was it worth it?

Once I realized that my husband continued to want someone else, I really wanted my life to end. One day after finding my husband at her house, I returned home determined to take all the medication I had in my possession. My husband arrived home and stopped me just before I tried to end my life.

Several years later, there was another couple with whom we played Andrew's sexual game. Staying at their cottage, my husband suggested we go swimming in the nude. I was recovering from surgery and could take showers, but was not yet able to submerge myself in water. When I whispered that it would not be good for me to go swimming in a lake he gave me the look that said, 'If you ruin this for me, you are going to pay for it.' I went ahead with his plan and we ended up playing Andrew's swapping game.

Is it normal for Christian married couples to do these things? Deep in my heart, I knew it was not.

On one occasion, that man came to my home and started kissing and touching me when my husband wasn't there. I made it clear to him that I had no interest in having sex with him. I was able to say no to him, but I never felt that brave with my husband.

The relationship with this couple also ended. My fear of Andrew did not allow me to suggest that swapping mates always ended the relationship.

The more disrespect my abuser showed to my body, the less and less of a human being I became. I was nothing more than a sex machine. Forced to do sexual acts I did not want to do, I was watching these acts from somewhere else as though it wasn't really me. The next day we never discussed it, and internally I pretended none of it had happened.

I occasionally hear in the news that women agree with their male partners to participate in horrific acts of rape, kidnapping, or sexual abuse. I often wonder if these women agree to participate in these immoral acts, because they are too afraid to say NO. Perhaps they are terrified of the consequences they would endure from their abuser.

There was a physical, emotional and spiritual price I paid because I did not run from the evil imposed on me. Over time, I hated myself more and more. I could not stand to look at myself in the mirror. Sometimes when I caught a glimpse of myself, I would think 'What a sinner! What a horrible person!' How could God ever forgive me?

I went through times when I stopped praying, reading my Bible, and relying on the power of the Holy Spirit. My integrity and relationship as a special child of God had disappeared.

Perhaps my faith could not save me after all.

A Life Filled With Shame

For years, I did not dare tell anyone about how my husband physically, emotionally or sexually abused me. What would people think of me if they knew how I was treated by him? I hid the bruises because I did not want his family, my family or anyone to know I was a wife who deserved to be beaten.

Why couldn't I get it right? I believed I was a failure and needed to try harder to make him happy. Why couldn't I learn what it took to be loved by my husband? In this farming community, good wives canned vegetables and fruits, made jam and pickles and ketchup and hung their clothes on the line. I did these things and yearned for approval from my husband. Would I ever make the level of the good wife?

Sometimes the bruises couldn't be hidden and I was asked, "What happened to you?" Then I would lie. I told them I stumbled into a doorway, fell down the steps, or caught my arm in the car door.

On a hot summer day, I was grocery shopping. Wearing shorts appropriate for the weather, I had forgotten the large bruise on the side of my leg. Taking my list, I put the items in the cart. After several inquisitive stares at my legs, I looked down, and I realized what had caught their eyes. I abandoned my cart, groceries and all, ran out of the store, jumped into my car, and sped home. I carried so much shame.

Many times, I was punched in my head, pushed into the wall, or hit by a thrown object. Later in life, diagnosing head pain and dizziness, my head was scanned and there were scars of this abuse.

Marriage vows are to love, cherish, comfort, honor and keep one another. Those words were used in our chapel ceremony as Andrew and I made a commitment to each other before God. Yet, they did not resemble our home at all.

"What God hath joined together, let no man put asunder," the minister said before pronouncing us husband and wife. Less than eight years later, I questioned what did those words mean? Did God really join us together? Was this what God had in mind for our marriage? Did the Reverend mean that no judge granting divorce could break this commitment? Didn't my husband put asunder or break our wedding vows every time he hit me, demeaned me or did awful things to my body?

Over and over, I recalled those words. I needed an explanation of what those words meant? I made an appointment with the Reverend. I wanted his opinion of how God looked at my abusive family life.

"What is the role of a Christian wife?" I asked him. I wondered how I could control my husband's anger that he took out on all three of us.

"What are you doing to make him so angry?" the Reverend asked. "Just stop making him angry."

I went home determined not to make him angry again.

Andrew told me everything that went wrong in our marriage, even with our sons, was my fault. If I did everything right, everything would be perfect. I took all of the blame. And now I had the Reverend saying that God did not want me to provoke

A Life Filled With Shame

my husband. Apparently, my husband had no responsibility for a happy marriage and family.

Andrew's father was a wonderful person. He was peaceful, loving, and kind. His admiration of me was evident and in desperation, I went to him.

"Can you help me, dad?" I asked. I showed him bruises on my arms. "Is there anything you can do?"

Promising he would talk to his son about the abusive behavior, I felt confident Andrew would listen to his dad. A couple days later, my father-in-law stopped by the house.

"I don't want to interfere with my son's marriage. I'm sure it will make him angry," he said. "I tried to find the words to bring it up to him, but I'm sorry. I just can't do it."

Once again I was alone and powerless to make him stop torturing the lives of my sons and me. Will I ever be free from the shame, blame and pain that keep me bound to him?

For many years, I never called my husband's behavior toward my sons and me as abuse. On my own, every day was another day of survival with the fear of what would make him mad. But as the saying goes, "One cannot see the forest through the trees."

I always worried. Would the boys inadvertently do something kid-like, and anger him?

Would I forget to put the toilet seat down? In Andrew's words, he did not want to look down that gaping hole. If I forgot to put it down, he would pick up the seat and slam it down, pick it up and slam it again.

Would I forget to close the bedroom closet door? He became very angry if the closet door was left open.

Or would he open the junk drawer only to dump the contents on the floor because he didn't agree with the concept of a junk drawer?

I would drive in the driveway and then contemplate; do I put the car in the garage, or leave it out on the driveway? Whatever I did, it seemed to be the wrong decision.

Before Andrew came home, I would see that everything was in its place. If I wouldn't make it home on time before he arrived, I would shake. Did I remember everything? What if I didn't? I would drive fast and careless trying to beat him home just to make sure all was well.

Still I never processed in my brain that it was abuse. It was as if I was brainwashed. All that changed one day while I was watching television. A silent advertisement flashed across the screen: Are you being abused?" The thought raced through my mind. Abuse! Was this abuse? Were we being abused? I think it is. This is abuse.

It wasn't that I couldn't do anything right, or that I was not trying hard enough, or praying enough, or not doing God's will. God was not punishing me. It was abuse, and the phone number of an abuse shelter appeared on the television screen. I called the number, and the receptionist asked if I could come in to speak with someone. I wanted to go, but first I had to make some kind of excuse to get the car, and someone to take care of the children so I could drive downtown to see a shelter counselor.

Living in a rural area, there was not a public bus for transportation. His control over me included a minimal opportunity to use our only car. Unless I had a proven need he would become argumentative when I asked to use it.

A Life Filled With Shame

Plus, driving in the city made me nervous. Where would I park? What if I had car problems? What if I had an accident? What if someone who knew me saw me downtown?

All of this was risky, because I did not want my husband to find out where I had gone. I was a wife who feared for her life to the extent that I did not want to anger him. It could cost me my life. However, I knew I had to seek help outside of the conservative church community where I lived. I had to begin somewhere.

I went to the shelter and met with a counselor. She told me it was risky for me and my sons not to seek safety. I wrestled with the decision of leaving my husband and taking my sons some place where we could be safe. I did not have a job, and I had not one ounce of confidence to go out and apply for one. Coming to the shelter was only a beginning and I was a long way from making this move. But it was a beginning. I knew in my heart that someday I would make the decision to leave.

In my heart and soul began the hope that someday I would be free. Every time he physically abused us, called us names, or belittled us, I thought to myself that someday, we would be free. This hope empowered me to face every day.

Is it possible my sons and I could survive the enemy?

A Struggle With My Faith

While I believed eventually we would escape, I struggled with my victim pathology that God approved of the abuse my sons and I were suffering. I came to believe in a punitive God who wanted us to suffer for some reason I could not determine.

After all, my conservative tradition taught me that a woman must honor submission to her husband. The scripture in *Ephesians 5.22 says, Wives, be subject to your husbands as you are to the Lord.*

Whatever Andrew wanted to do to me, either physically, emotionally, or sexually had to be accepted. Wasn't that what the scripture said?

For the wife does not rule over her own body, but the husband does. I Corinthians 7:3

I believed in the sanctity of marriage and the covenant I had made with my husband. Our marriage covenant had been broken by Andrew who had promised to love, honor and cherish me. He not only broke these vows by the physical abuse but also by the inappropriate behavior he forced upon me with other men.

For years I prayed God would change him and believed that at any minute God would zap him. Then my husband would realize his abusive behavior was not acceptable. It was as though I was bound to scripture but my husband was not held accountable to God. Yet, *Ephesians 5:21 says, Be subject to one another out of reverence for Christ.* Each must respect one another. I must respect him, and he must respect me.

A Struggle With My Faith

Later I learned that the marriage relationship was compared to Christ's relationship with his church. *Ephesians 5.23 says, For the husband is the head of the wife just as Christ is the head of the church. Just as Christ gave his life for his church, so the husband should be willing to give his life for his wife.* This was not the atmosphere in our home.

We still had a marriage license valid in the eyes of the state, but did God regard our marriage as valid? The conservative church community preached against divorce unless adultery could be proven. Does the sexual assault and abuse in our home meet the qualifications of adultery?

I was too blinded by the confines of a religious institution to seek the truth.

I was so torn, and the freedom to voice my opinion of what was scripturally, spiritually, or morally right or wrong did not belong to me.

Spurned by the obsession of wanting to do God's will and the fear of making God angry, I made an appointment with the Christian Counseling Service in a neighboring town. I begged the male counselor to give me the permission to leave my husband.

"Please tell me what God wants me to do?" I said. "I need an answer to come down from heaven in black and white so I know that what I do is God's will."

Instead of giving me the permission I needed, the Christian Counselor quoted scripture about anger and "not letting the sun set on one's anger." I never did understand whose anger he was talking about. Andrew's or mine? Nothing the Christian Counselor said gave me hope. Confused and disappointed, I did not return.

After that appointment, I drove into my driveway with anxiety causing my breathing to be in short gasps and spasms in my stomach.

Would my husband be home already? Would he check the mileage? Would he notice I did not have a package when I was supposed to be shopping?

The guilt of doing something behind his back made me shake. I was not a confident liar.

Although I sought confirmation of God's will, I wondered if there was a God for me. My prayers were not being answered. There were days and weeks and sometimes even months when I could not pray. Why bother since they were not answered anyway?

God had abandoned me.

My Lost Love

During this difficult time of severe abuse, low self esteem, and doubt about the presence of God, I heard from my high school sweetheart and first love, Lee. He called and asked about my life.

"I think about you all the time," he said. He told me he was still in love with me and had never forgotten about me, even when he fought in the Vietnam War and was injured. Married with two children, his marriage was rocky with several separations.

It was easy for me to believe he still cared for me. Lee was a gentle and kind man and his attention felt good. Having someone talk to me with kind words and an understanding heart was wonderful.

We began talking every day and eventually met one another on back roads for an hour here or there. It wasn't easy because my husband never stayed home alone with the boys. Therefore, I would hire a babysitter in order to be free to steal a few moments to meet my high school sweetheart.

Lee had dumped me in high school and broke my heart without a single word of explanation. Yet that red flag of memory never entered my thoughts.

I was convinced Lee cared deeply for me so it was easy for me to love him. He loved me, and he would never be abusive to me. He promised me he would always respect me. I thrived on the attention.

Shame Shame Go Away!

Since I lived with the shame of perverted sexual acts from Andrew, I already felt like a guilty sinner. Now another sin was added for which I was guilty. I knew it was a sin for me to be emotionally involved with another man.

I felt too guilty to face God so more and more I withdrew from the presence of the Lord. I couldn't talk to God or beg Him for deliverance. As a Christian wife and mother, the shame of my sin separated me from God. How could God ever forgive me?

Feeling abandoned by God, I made excuses for my behavior to try to make it right. I told myself my husband didn't value me. Why would he care what emotions I had for another man?

But no matter how hard I tried, deep in my heart I did not believe my attachment to my high school sweetheart was justified. I could not judge what my husband deserved or did not deserve however I did judge myself. I had fallen from grace as a spiritual wife and mother and I felt full of shame. For months, I argued with my conscience.

Yet this secret relationship with Lee was my power over my life. It was one tiny bit of power in a powerless marriage.

Lee asked me to leave my husband so I could be safe. But I was married to an abusive husband who would never let me get a divorce so I could be free to marry another man. NO WAY!

"I can't do it. I don't dare. It would be dangerous," I told Lee. "You don't know how dangerous it is to live with Andrew."

Lee and I wanted a future together. He promised me a normal life, which I desperately wanted but I was too scared to pursue happiness. Yet, my relationship with Lee gave me hope for the future in my hopeless world.

My Lost Love

It wasn't until much later I learned God was present for me. I just couldn't feel the Divine with my back turned.

A Trial Run

Our family was friends with a family of four sons, and we visited their home often. With our two boys there were six boys under 12 running through the house. Drinking coffee and chatting was a challenge. Our son, Mark, did not do anything naughty, but he was the one my husband targeted to express his power. Andrew shoved Mark's head repeatedly against the cupboard in their home – bam – bam – bam. My 10-year-old had tears in his eyes not only from the pain but also from humiliation.

"You wimp! What a baby!" his father said to him. Crying was not permitted in our family.

What must it have felt like to have his father care so little that he was willing to hit and embarrass him in front of his friends?

As his mother, I wanted to take Mark in my arms and stroke his head. Yet, I did nothing because I did not dare to offer a hug or a kind word.

Something happened to me that night, though. Feeling helpless to defend myself or my sons, the end of the line had come.

After we returned home from what had begun as a fun night with friends, lying in bed with my husband I planned our escape, rehearsing it in my mind what I would have to do.

Morning came and I got up as usual. By now, I had my own car so I removed my car key from Andrew's ring and made him breakfast. I then went to my husband who was still lying in bed, and proceeded with the getting-up-routine. First, I put his socks on him and then his underwear as he lifted his butt for me to pull

A Trial Run

them up. I pulled his t-shirt over his head and continued to dress this 230-pound man as he lay in bed, still snoozing. After my coaxing, he angrily got up to eat the breakfast I had made him. This had been the ritual for 13 years.

He left for work and I put my plan into action. I went to the grocery store, picked up some boxes, came home and packed the bare necessities, as fast as possible. My husband came home every day for lunch. The kids and I had to be out of there before he came home.

The kids wanted to take the dog.

"No, not the dog," I said with anger. "Leave him to take care of that darn dog. But we can take the fish."

I had called my sister in a nearby town, told her of the circumstances, and she insisted we stay with her. I threw a cot in the trunk. One of the kids could sleep on it. On second thought, I threw it out on the grass. How would I explain to my sister why the cot had a perfectly round hole cut into it? It was a hole my husband had made for one of his perverted sexual fantasies.

I left him a note, 'Cannot take it any more so we have left.'

As I drove away, something I had dreamed about doing for many years, I felt fear, but I also felt free. I did not look back in my rear view mirror.

We were safe at least for the moment. We began a new life, living with my sister in a nearby town. Every day I drove the kids to the school in our old town as I wanted them to have a stable life without having to change schools.

I did not have income so I went to my parents for help. I told them about the last 13 years of my life and the terrifying nightmare of fear my sons and I lived every day. I had kept the way my husband treated our sons and me a secret from them. They promised their support, both psychologically and financially. They helped me retain an attorney to file for divorce.

However, my security and safety were short lived. The attorney insisted that the boys and I needed to move back into the family home. When the divorce papers were filed, I would be granted at least temporary possession of the home. I shared my concern about the safety of going back into the home. I wanted safety not property.

"Have the police number flashing by your phone. You live in a rural area, and it will take a while for police protection to arrive," the attorney said. "He won't leave you alone – guaranteed. I am concerned for your safety, too."

The attorney obtained an order from the judge for my husband to vacate the family home. My sons and I would need to occupy the home immediately. Andrew must have been expecting such an order, because he had a full-size flatbed trailer loaded with everything he could pack ready to roll when he vacated the family home.

The judge signed a restraining order for our protection and my husband was not allowed on the property. I knew that would really upset Andrew since no one would tell him what he could or couldn't do. Obeying rules and laws were not his priority. He believed everything belonged to him; therefore sharing possessions with me was unlikely. He felt no responsibility to provide his kids with a place to live.

Returning to our hometown area, I no longer felt the safety of living with my sister in another town. I was back in the religious conservative community that did not allow divorces and

A Trial Run

where wives were to be submissive to their husbands regardless of how they were treated.

When the faith community learned I had filed for divorce, they voiced judgment rather than love and support. They ignored me, gave me judgmental looks, or whispers behind my back. For those who did speak to me, their words were not realistic.

"Keep praying."

"Accept Jesus as your Savior, and he will help you."

"Keep the commandments."

Moreover, from the few, who accepted the truth about the abuse, I heard,

"The Bible says you must forgive."

These simple misinterpretations contributed to my guilt, self-blame, and suffering. The church used the Bible to excuse or justify his abuse.

There was no understanding by the Reverend or the Christian community on the dynamics of family abuse. As long as my family maintained a façade of normalcy, the community believed that for better or for worse until death do us part' meant 'stay in the marriage no matter what.' My church family had let me down. They did not know the years of prayerful discernment before the difficult decision to pursue safety for my sons and me.

Night after night, I stayed awake in fear that Andrew would disregard the restraining order and break into the house in a rage. I slept with a knife under my pillow. Everywhere I went I was looking in my rear view mirror.

Andrew violated the order and visited the children on the school playground.

"You miss me, don't ya?" he said. "Ask mom if I can come back home."

When I presented the restraining order to the principal of our elementary school, he said, "I hope you will reconsider getting a divorce. It would be so sad if the boys had to live without a dad."

Frustrated, I left the school, realizing that no matter how much truth I told about the physical and psychological abuse, very few people would believe me.

What would be the next step my husband would take to gain power and control over his family?

I Have Found Jesus!

My husband had a religious upbringing that exposed him to Christianity. He had been raised in the church, attended Sunday school and catechism classes, and was educated in the Christian School.

Yet when the kids and I left him, he chose that particular time in his life to find Jesus. With a Bible in his hand, he visited our pastor, his family of origin, and our friends.

"Through prayer, God forgave me and my life is changed," he told everyone he visited. Faced with the possibility of losing his wife and sons, he had become a born again Christian, and wanted to live a new life in Christ.

Our friends and his family called and shared with me how he wanted another chance. One of his friends said as my husband talked about his born again experience, he became angry I had filed for divorce. He pounded on his windshield, causing it to crack. It was a reminder of the times he cracked my windshields in anger.

For years, I had been praying that God would speak to his heart so his behavior would change. I wanted to believe he had changed.

I knew Jesus' instruction regarding forgiveness in *Luke 17.3-4: Be on your guard. If another disciple sins, you must rebuke the offender, and if there is repentance, you must forgive.*

Therefore, when my husband appeared one night at the family home, even though I had a restraining order which said he could not come on the property, he convinced me to let him in. He said he talked to the police chief in the small town we lived, and the restraining order was ineffective.

"It's just a piece of paper," he said. "My name is on the title of the home too, so I'm allowed on the property." I believed him.

He asked if I had received a card he sent me. I was so impressed he had given me anything that I blushed. He used his kind words to manipulate me and instead of being firm and refusing to converse with him, we talked together. But I never confronted his abusive behavior.

I never said to him, 'When you hit the kids, or throw things or threaten us, it scares us. We live in fear. When you make me do horrible sex acts, it makes me feel like a whore. I cannot live with any of this anymore.'

Never making him accountable for his behavior was a mistake. I was shocked he wasn't screaming at me for filing for divorce so I believed he had a change of heart. However, I heard no mention of taking the responsibility for the 13 years of the hellish existence we called our family. I let him off the hook and offered him cheap grace.

He professed he had been saved. There was no repentance to God for violating his marriage vows or abusing his children. Repentance refers to turning around, a change of self. *Repent and turn from all your sins. Get yourself a new heart and a new spirit. Turn, then and live. Ezekiel 18.30-32.* There was none of that kind of repentance.

A few days earlier, I had received a visit from the pastor and another church officer.

I Have Found Jesus!

"If you are not open to reconciliation with your husband to save your marriage, the Sacrament of Holy Communion will not be offered to you next Sunday," they said. I remembered how important it had been for me to join the church, to be part of the congregation, and to participate in the Sacrament of Holy Communion.

The church had abandoned me and if the church abandoned me, perhaps my Lord had also abandoned me. The church leaders made it clear to me that it was my responsibility to forgive Andrew. It was my part of bringing him to salvation. I did not feel I had another option. This was God's will to save my marriage, right?

I thought that maybe I just had to endure the suffering of living with him to keep the family together. Jesus suffered, and he was the model for suffering. The Bible talked about having a cross to bear. Did this mean my cross to bear was to forgive a man whose abusive behavior had stomped the hearts and spirits in the lives of his family?

Searching my heart, I questioned if I was capable of loving him again. Had my love turned to hate? Was my heart completely empty? I was so confused; yet, in less than two weeks, he moved back into our home. I didn't tell him he could, he just did it. I immediately dropped the divorce proceedings.

The church minister had suggested marital therapy, and my husband agreed. Together we attended three therapy sessions with a Christian counselor. Each week before we left home, he told me what to say and according to him, "We will not be talking with the counselor about anything else." Of course, I complied. I was still his puppet with no voice. I knew better than to even hint at the physical, emotional, or sexual abuse.

"What happens in our marriage is private," he said to me. I did not want to upset the apple cart, and I knew better than to make him angry.

After my husband and others convinced me that God expected me to forgive him, I terminated my relationship with Lee. I was going to put my heart and soul into my marriage. With sincerity and commitment, I asked God to forgive me. When I felt forgiveness, I felt a heavy weight lifted off my heart.

I went into our marriage reconciliation with a clear conscience and a commitment to work on being a good Christian wife.

To reward me for giving the marriage another chance, my husband bought us a new bedroom suite, new wedding rings, and within a few months, a different house. Andrew wanted us to have a fresh start.

I believed the reconciliation of my marriage was God's will, or was it?

After The Reconciliation

For the next three years, he was careful with the physical abuse and did not leave bruises. He still was demeaning, demanding, controlling and there was always the fear of the threat of the unknown. Sexually he continued to force me to have sex in ways that caused pain not pleasure.

Behind my back, he continued to abuse our sons. I worked outside the home so he was there alone with them. After losing his temper, he would hit or kick them and threaten them with further abuse if they told me about it. My sons believed him and never told me or showed me what their father had done to them.

One day I came home from work and found blood all over the three-season porch. No one was there. Imagining what might have happened; I jumped in the car, and sped off to the family doctor. My husband and sons were not there. I returned home and paced the floor for hours, waiting for their return.

Michael had not picked up some branches in the yard, so Andrew had slammed a door on our son's fingers, breaking the skin and necessitating stitches. He did not take Michael to the community doctor, but rather to the hospital emergency room where there would be fewer questions.

"Do not tell your mother how this happened," his dad told him. Quizzing him before they returned home on the made-up story of the accident, Michael did as he was told. The true story came out much later.

Shame Shame Go Away!

To Andrew's credit, he was full of ideas for family vacations. The boys were at a perfect age to travel and Andrew decided we would rent a motor home and take a spring break trip to the nation's capital. He suggested we take my sister, a single mom, and her child with us.

We left in the early evening, and decided to travel all night to save time. My husband, sister and me, sat together in the cab. After a few hours on the road, the three children had fallen asleep in the back and we stopped at a truck stop. While my sister was in the bathroom, my husband, who was always turned on by her, told me that he wanted this opportunity to play around with her. My instructions were to say I was tired, and then climb into the bunk over the cab. He would then be free to fondle my sister. I argued with him, but felt powerless.

Reluctantly I followed his plan. I had might as well have delivered my sister to my sick and abusive husband on a platter. As I lay in the bunk above the cab, tears soaked my pillow. I had deceived her, and was reminded once again of the control Andrew had over me. I felt unworthy and filled with shame. When we stopped for breakfast, my sister and I did not speak about the incident. However, when I looked into her eyes, I believed I saw not only fear but empathy for me.

Arriving in Washington, D.C. late morning, Andrew was not prepared for driving a huge motor home in heavy traffic without available parking. He became erratic, drove carelessly, and verbally assaulted me because I could not read the map to help us find a place to park.

There was a cloud of tension in the vehicle as I tried to get us out of harm's way. I knew I had to find a safe place for all of us

After The Reconciliation

so we could re-group. I found a visitor's center to help us locate a place to park the motor home.

Remembering the fear I saw in my sister's eyes from my husband's assault, I asked her to come along. In a panic, we ran up the walkway, and asked the attendant for camping suggestions. As the attendant was giving us information, I tried to emphasize the importance of finding a campground with complete directions on how to get there. She read the location from a handbook.

"You don't understand. I need perfect directions on how to get there. It's very important." I needed to know how far to go, where to turn and the name of the road. I also needed to know the cost for the campground.

My heart was racing and my head was pounding. Lord, help me get it right. My sister helped me remember the details, and we were able to find the safety of a campground.

Once there, we were relieved that Andrew's fit of rage had subsided at least for that day. However, there was this cloud of tension throughout the remainder of the vacation.

Being employed helped me gain confidence and skills. Armed with this, I set a goal for our freedom from the chains of power and control held by this evil man. I was determined to become independent as I could no longer deny what was happening to my sons while I was at work. Once I realized they were being terrorized by their father, I questioned him on his behavior toward them. Unlike the many years before where I hid while he abused them, I began to defend them.

Telling him I would not stand for his abusing them was a huge step for me. Did it anger him? Absolutely, but I didn't care.

I wanted out and this time I would be ready, psychologically and financially. I felt empowered to stand up for our rights. This did not happen overnight, in a few weeks or even months. It was three years before I was strong enough to say to him, "I don't want you to live here anymore. I want you to get out. I have no love for you. I have no feelings for you whatsoever, nothing."

Empowering me to take this step were other circumstances that entered the picture.

The Last Straw

"You're just jealous," Andrew said. "She's nothing more than a friend, that's all."

This woman friend lived near his employment and for well over a year, the friendship between my husband and this woman continued. I wanted to believe him when he denied any indiscretion. Some days he even convinced me it was my fault for accusing him.

However, when he didn't come right home after work, I would drive by her house, and his car would be there. After months and months of stopping regularly at her home after work, I began another conversation with Andrew.

"Why was your car in her garage? What are you trying to hide? Why is her friendship so important to you?"

He continued to deny anything was going on. In defense of his friendship theory, Andrew suggested we get together with her and her husband, who worked long hours and was often away from home. Against my better judgment, I went along with developing a friendship with them on a social basis.

When we entertained with this couple, there were always looks between Andrew and the younger woman, casual touching between them, and I witnessed them playing footsie under the table. When my husband flirted with her, he treated her different than he did me. Once again, I felt not good enough, not thin enough and not sexy enough to keep his interest.

Shame Shame Go Away!

Even my sons noticed the attention their father showed to her.

When he was stranded at her house in a snowstorm one night with her husband working, ten-year-old Michael said, "You might as well admit it, Mom. He likes her more than you."

Andrew badgered me to befriend her and take up golfing, so I could go golfing with her. She was very petite, so I lost weight, attempting to be the same size. I wanted him to look at me not her.

Trying to convince myself I wasn't exaggerating their involvement, I started to record all of the doubts I had about my husband and his relationship with this woman. Over a year's time, I had pages and pages of dates and events. I was angry over how he had mistreated me for over 16 years; yet his needs were being met by this woman.

The day arrived when I could take no more. As I looked at him, I thought of his abuse, humiliation, and degradation towards my sons and me. I no longer felt any emotion toward him. I wanted him out of my life.

"I don't want you here anymore," I said. "Get out."

After years and years of terror as well as the need for freedom from his power and control, I had gained the strength to say, "I'm done."

He moved out. Nevertheless, because I knew the evil he was capable of inflicting, I remained fearful of him. However, he did stay away, and I filed for divorce. Andrew had made a negative impact on the lives of all three of us for too long.

The Last Straw

Not long thereafter, he committed himself to a Christian Mental Health Hospital. I believed he knew I would not accept his finding Jesus again to get back into the family's home.

"Your husband gave me permission to call and ask if you would come into the hospital and talk about your marriage," the mental health professional asked. "Will you come in and talk with me?"

"Only if Andrew is not present," I said.

The following day I met with Andrew's psychologist at the mental health facility.

"Your husband is requesting marital therapy," the psychologist said. "Are you willing to participate in counseling?"

"Let me tell you about my life," I said.

For the next three hours I told him about all of the physical violence and emotional battering to our sons, as well as the abuse and sexual assault on me. I did not leave out a single act of craziness Andrew created in our lives.

"Well, this is your side of the story," Andrew's psychologist said. "Now let's listen to his story. He says that he has had a lot of pressure with his job."

Rage burned inside as I got out of the chair and shook my finger in his face.

"This is not about his job," I said. "This is not something I dreamed up before I got here. This has been my life. This has been the hell my kids and I have gone through." I took a breath. "His job? I'm not interested in a story about his job. Sixteen years of living with the insanity of this man is long enough for me."

I left the facility. There would be no therapy and no reconciliation.

Shame Shame Go Away!

With that decision, we were given a chance to live.

Freedom from Fear?

After I had left my husband for the first time, filed for divorce, and took him back, I had changed. I had procured a job and gained respect in the conservative community where we lived. I was empowered.

I felt deserving of respect and wanted a divorce. I was no longer going to allow the church to deter me from following through with my desire to find a safe environment for my sons and for me. They were 13 and 11 years old, and I wanted to give them a stable life.

I had resumed my relationship with Lee during my divorce proceedings and carefully introduced him into the lives of my sons. Given their violent childhood, I did not know how they would respond. However, they were like sponges for the attention Lee gave them. He was interested and excited to be a role model for them. I was grateful I had Lee, whose presence in our lives gave us protection.

Andrew signed himself out of the mental hospital as soon as he was told I would be filing for divorce. He began stalking me by driving by the house. One morning when I got up, there was a bullet hole through the picture window.

He arrived at the house late one night after the boys were in bed and was pounding on the door. "Open the door!" he yelled. I dialed 911 in the dark as I sat on the floor of the dinette.

"I need an officer here right away. My estranged husband is trying to get in," I told the emergency operator. Andrew left after a time when I did not respond to his demands. The police never did arrive.

My desire for a new life with Lee strengthened my resolve to move forward with the divorce. It took every bit of confidence not to buckle under the guilt and shame dished out to me from my soon to be ex-husband, along with the church community where it still was not socially or religiously acceptable to get a divorce.

Righteous people I knew for almost 20 years ignored me. Some knew about the abuse but did not seem to care. Their interpretation of the Bible was that divorce was an unforgiveable sin.

God must have told them it was so, since they acted as though it was their responsibility to judge me, convict me and sentence me to hell. I felt shame, but I wasn't worried about hell. I had already suffered the torments of hell by living through abuse in every imaginable way.

Leaving the court hearing that finalized my divorce, I drove back home, still fearing Andrew would jump out at me, or run me off the road. Living with fear for so many years, to be free seemed like an illusion.

Trying to buy my freedom from fear, I fashioned the divorce settlement to favor Andrew. No longer legally attached to him, still I did not want to anger him. Therefore, I borrowed $5,000 to give him, like a bribe, as part of the settlement, hoping he would leave the kids and me alone. Winning was important to Andrew so I let him think he won. My truth was that we were free, so we were the true winners.

Free From Fear?

But we weren't free. Andrew's presence in our lives did not stop when the divorce was final. Not only because Andrew had visitation of our sons, but also we weren't free from the presence of the shame and pain caused by the violence. My guilt of failing to protect my sons from their father's abuse remained with me. Cleansing the shame took another three decades.

Andrew continued to blame me for the divorce, and never admitted the truth of how he treated his family. Without assuming responsibility for his actions, he has never been held accountable for his behavior.

Not surprising, Andrew brags to his sons and grandchildren about the wonderful life he gave his family. He proudly tells his memories of the happy lives he gave his sons in their childhood. When my sons hear these stories, they still do not possess the confidence to confront him about the truth of their childhood.

Until he is held accountable and Andrew hears the truth, the journey of my sons' healing can never be complete.

Regardless, my sons and I sought the good life.

My Second Chance for Happiness

Five weeks after my divorce was final, Lee and I were married in a sacred ceremony where we promised our personal vows in the presence of God. My two children and Lee's two children participated in the ceremony. Each of us held a candle as we blended two families into one.

We were thrilled with a second chance for love. While we thought our love was like being in heaven, our community thought we were hell bound. It was like being served a warrant, declared guilty, and sentenced without the gift of grace.

My ex-husband, Andrew, brought us a book as a wedding gift entitled, <u>What To Do To Avoid Being Bored in Bed</u>. However, Lee and I did not allow his poor taste to ruin the beginning of a loving marriage.

For the first time in my life, a man intimately loved me. He showed me love by having normal desire for me, like a man who wants a woman. He desired me without demeaning me. He respected my body by not causing me pain as he made love to me. I would never have to worry about being forced to do something that was repulsive.

We were convinced God's forgiveness flowed over and through us. We were going to live our married life, putting God first. As a family, we attended church every Sunday together and I was truly pleased.

My Second Chance for Happiness

We had decided that our family of his two children and my two children (ages 10, 11, 12 and 13) would be our focus. It was a houseful and a handful.

My sons loved their step-dad and having fun as a family with their new stepsister and brother. They experienced the freedom to play ball in the yard without the fear of reprimand for stepping on the blades of their father's grass.

There were no words for the happiness in my heart. Lee showed me his love in so many ways. I had never been loved like this before. My chains released, I was free, and the lightness within me made me want to smile at everyone.

Within six months, we decided to move out of the conservative community. Wanting a fresh start with my new husband and family, I sold the home awarded me in the divorce. Together we bought 20 acres in a nearby community and started to plan our beautiful home in the country where our two young teens and two pre-teens would have lots of space to roam. As I drove out of town, I never looked back. A different environment was healthy for the kids and me.

Lee was such a beautiful person; kind, considerate, gentle, and the most affectionate man I had ever known. Everyone who met or knew him loved him. Feeling as though I had won the lottery, I was determined to be the very best wife and mother. Moreover, I would take the covenant of our marriage very seriously.

Accustomed to being told I was a good cook, I made meals that included meat, potatoes, vegetables, and dessert. Trained by their father to eat in silence without making the choice of what they liked or wanted, my sons ate everything that was placed in front of them.

This was not the case with my new stepfamily. The first delicious meal I proudly served to my new family of six was interrupted with the tears of the 10- year-old step-son.

"There isn't anything here that I can eat," he whispered to his dad. I was then informed that there was a list of five things he ate: breakfast cereal, macaroni and cheese, hot dogs, spaghetti, and sloppy joes, made exactly like his mother did. And that was it. Insecure in my new role of a step-mom, I was hurt. Fighting tears, I made yet another vow to do what I had to do to endear myself to my new step-kids. Meal planning was going to be a challenge.

Lee's kids and mine thrown together in a blended family didn't just happen. I found a support group in a neighboring town which met on a week night entitled, Forming the Healthy Blended Family. Living the amazing second chance for happiness was not going to be easy.

The memories of living as a battered woman penetrated my thoughts. Even moving out of the house I shared with my ex and out of the community did not remove the re-runs in my mind. Just seeing abuse reminded me of what the horrors had been for me.

Remembering the physical, verbal, and sexual abuse kept me a victim even though I had this wonderful new husband and life. Often I took something my new husband said the wrong way and my feelings were hurt very easy. I jumped if he lifted his hand. I talked to him about my abusive marriage, but he didn't appear interested. Before we were married, he was more understanding about my past.

"You talk about your past too much," my friend told me. "He doesn't want to hear about it."

After that conversation, every time I thought about another trauma in our lives, I stuffed it deeper and deeper. It took some training on my part and many times I would start to say something and stopped. I tried to forget as others told me to do.

"Just forget it and move on. That was in the past," friends told me.

I couldn't. I had not even begun to heal from my previous life and had no right to pursue another relationship, let alone a marriage with children.

Our entire life was focused on the four kids. My husband worked the second shift so we only had weekends together and little privacy for the two of us. We filled weekends with activities so the kids would feel the bonding we had hoped would happen. I didn't mind sharing him with the kids.

There were issues to say the least. My stepdaughter was jealous of her dad's affection towards me. She often insisted on sleeping on our bedroom floor. Gifts that Lee bought me sometimes disappeared, and later I found them in her closet. I suggested Lee give her individual time, taking her out for breakfast or giving her special favors. I did not feel I was competing with her. He could love her and me at the same time. At times I felt frustrated with her behavior but I loved her as though she were my own daughter. I hoped that someday she would feel different towards me. My stepson was affectionate, treated me with respect, and brought me great joy.

Shame Shame Go Away!

On Friday nights and weekends when Lee was home, all the kids adored him. Lee was their hero, and they placed him on a pedestal as they competed for his attention. Discipline was not necessary when he was around. I loved to see how my sons responded to their step-dad's positive reinforcement.

I needed help with his presence in the evening. I begged him to ask for a different shift but he didn't seem to understand how important that was to me.

If I could hang in there and get the kids raised, I was convinced the two of us would have the happy life we longed to live.

I continued to attempt to transition everyone into one happy family. It was difficult because there were two sets of house rules and expectations; his and mine. I believe Lee and I gave it our best effort to treat all of the kids the same, but it felt normal for us to favor our own flesh and blood. When there was conflict, he took the side of his kids, just as I took the side of mine.

Every evening I had to beat it home from work, because Lee was at work. Since he wasn't around in the evening, it was my responsibility to attend school events, open houses, and attend little league games. Six innings of three different ball games in varying locations after a full day of work became tiresome. We lived out in the country and often the kids needed transportation to school events, so I became the Mom taxi.

"This is my real mom," my stepdaughter said as she introduced her mother to her friend at a ballgame once. It was one of the lessons in my role as a step-mom. I would never replace the real mom. Yet one night I wondered where her real mom was when she was in pain after having her tonsils out and I sat alone by her bed because her dad was deer hunting.

My Second Chance for Happiness

Lee and I had very little time to discuss important decisions together. He came home from work after I had gone to bed. I wanted to wait up for him, but I had to get up early in the morning to get the kids off to school and leave for my job. When he hopped into bed, we had small talk, but nothing of great importance for which I had longed.

For the first time in my life, I felt safe and confident enough to express my opinion about making decisions. Lee listened as I gave my opinions on various issues, but especially financial decisions. However, to my surprise, as if he had not even considered my opinion, he would go ahead and make the decision he wanted.

"We are not on the same channel, same radio, but different frequencies," I would sometimes say to him.

I'll do better, I said to myself when Lee told me I had a negative attitude on life. I would be less negative and more positive. But I found it wasn't easy. Life often felt overwhelming. My mother had been so negative throughout my childhood and I hoped her negativity had not rubbed off on me.

Starving for Lee's attention, I shared him with not only the kids but his widowed mother. In the first year of our marriage, Lee was hospitalized in traction for three or four weeks. Besides a full-time job and handling all the home responsibilities, I was at the hospital every morning before work at 7 a.m. to help him eat breakfast. Then I returned after work to help him with dinner. To avoid paying for parking at the hospital, I parked down a side street and walked for my twice-daily visits and back again. Most of the days, I was exhausted.

When the hospital issued each patient a free parking pass, Lee told me he had given it to his 60-year-old mother, who also visited him every day. I felt diminished, unappreciated and angry and told him. He called me by his ex's name, and I went over the edge.

"You're always so negative," he yelled as I walked out of the hospital room.

He was right.

I had never processed or healed from my 16-year abusive marriage. I had unexpressed anger that had turned into depression, although I could not identify its presence at the time. Moreover, I had not sought counseling or medication for my depression.

Processing my past and overwhelmed with my present, it was difficult to be positive.

Where Is The Justice?

I could not wash my hands of my ex-husband as I had wished. I had asked my attorney to limit visitation, but the judge awarded Andrew visitation every other weekend. My sons did not want to spend entire weekends with their father but were willing to visit him for the day. Since Andrew did not want to drive out to the country to pick them up, I brought them to his house just to accommodate him.

The divorce decree gave him the right to see my sons, and intimidated, I worried he would take me back to court if I encouraged my sons to not see him. The boys did not want him to know what was going on in their lives. The less he knew the less he would find fault with them so they told him very little. I felt guilty that I left him out of their lives as much as I did, but knew Andrew would use it against us the more he knew.

While they were in therapy, the therapist told me they had the right to say they did not want to see their dad as much. Eventually my sons no longer visited him.

It seemed to me that Andrew still wanted control over me and I think he sensed my fear of him. Was it the way I shook or refused eye contact when I talked to him? Or the way I wanted to please him? I still did not want to make him upset. He was unpredictable and never knowing what would come next with him always kept me off guard. He continued to seek ways to have some connection with me.

Shame Shame Go Away!

And as unbelievable as it was, I still craved his approval. Just one little ounce of approval could make me a good person. I did not have loving feelings for him, but he still owned my self-esteem.

As long as my ex-husband had a wife or was dating another woman, he left me alone. But when his marriage or relationship fell through, he would start following me or just show up some place where I was. He often reminded me that I was a terrible mother, and doing a horrible job of raising his sons.

My youngest son loved the feeling of a sleeping bag versus sheets and blankets on his bed. I didn't insist he sleep in a sleeping bag but neither did I demand that he sleep on the sheets. I let him make the choice, and he desired to sleep in the bag. Somehow my ex-husband found out.

"You don't have any control over the kids," he said. "Put your foot down and demand he get under the covers." As far as I was concerned, it wasn't important enough to make an issue.

Afraid he would find out through others that our son was being confirmed in the church where my ex had connections, I invited him to attend the service. I thought I was being considerate, but it turned out to be a huge mistake. I let my son choose what he wore at that service. He usually only wore t-shirts, but on this occasion he wore a button-down dress shirt with dress pants and shoes, but no suit jacket or sweater. It was quite a feat for me to get him to agree to this dress-up image, let alone anything different. After the service, Andrew harassed me because our 14-year-old son, in his opinion, was dressed inappropriately for the occasion. He stated that I had no control over our sons, and should not have custody of them.

Where Is The Justice?

But he didn't let it go at that. He would show up at night while my husband was at work. I felt like he was watching me wherever I went. Once before when this was going on, he ran me off the road when I wouldn't pull over. Therefore Lee contacted police authorities to be in my work parking lot both in the morning and at the close of day.

One Friday night after work, I left my office and walked behind the building to my car. I was looking into my purse for my keys, when from behind two parked cars, my ex-husband jumped out at me. He had been waiting for me and I knew this is not going to be good.

Where were the police? They had promised they would be here just as a visual reminder to Andrew that they were watching, yet they were nowhere to be seen. My ex-husband started to harass me about the inappropriate clothing Michael had worn for confirmation.

"After all, that's why I send you money every week." he yelled.

I knew I had to get into my car where I would be safe, but I couldn't find my keys.

His anger was at a boiling point because I was ignoring him. When a warning button inside of me said, make a break for it, I ran back into the law office. I almost made it to the rear office door, which was locked. I fell on my hands and knees and the contents of my opened purse fell onto the sidewalk. I scrambled to get to my feet, trying to pick up the contents of my purse, as he kicked at my legs, cursing as he assaulted me.

This was happening at 5 p.m. on a Friday on the busiest street in town. The light was red and the cars were stopped yet not a

Shame Shame Go Away!

soul came to my rescue. No one stopped their car, and no one rolled down their window and yelled, "What's going on?" But they were watching. Some looked and then looked away. Some looked and their eyes met mine as I screamed, "Help me." I will never forget those eyes, but no rescue attempt.

I found my keys on the ground, limped to the door and he ran away. I fumbled getting the door open, but once I reached safety, I yelled for one of my bosses. Sobbing, I told them what had happened.

"I'm calling the cops," I said as I dialed 911. "They were supposed to be here." After calling the police, I sat down to get my breath and then went into the rest room to wipe my scraped knees.

The police arrived right away and knew my employers as I worked for attorneys in this conservative community.

After talking in depth with the cops and my bosses, they convinced me not to file charges against Andrew. The police promised they would pay him a visit and give him a warning.

"That should be sufficient," they said.

Would justice ever be on my side? It seemed that married or divorced my ex-husband would never be held accountable for what he did to me.

Expecting legal advice from the attorneys where I worked, I wondered why they did not support me. But these attorneys were members of the conservative church that glorified men as having power over the women in their lives. These same attorneys demanded I wore a skirt and heels every day. Within a month from this incident, the law firm told me that they no longer needed my services.

Where Is The Justice?

Threatened by this incident with my ex-husband and always on guard, I wondered if I would ever break the chains of fear.

Moreover, his child support payments were sporadic and the court system at that time did not issue warrants when fathers fell behind in payments. Unless the mother of the children really pursued the court, the Friend of the Court did nothing to claim unpaid child support, and I would do nothing to disrupt the life of my previous abusive spouse.

I left him alone so perhaps he would leave us alone too.

My Life Falls Apart

One very important part I envisioned in my new marriage was sharing our spiritual lives together. A short time following our marriage, my husband found one excuse after another not to attend church with me. While we dated, the whole family, all six of us, had attended church together.

On Saturdays, I would initiate the conversation of attending church.

"You choose where you want to go. I'm open to attend anywhere," I said. "I think it's important for the kids."

Refusing to communicate why he felt so different about attending church, it became a huge barrier between us.

Consequently, the young teenage children also refused to go with me. After all, if dad didn't go why should they have to go? I was very disappointed that he refused to even talk with me about the situation.

An important part of my soul was empty and I felt ignored but I decided to stop bringing it up. More important for me at the time was raising our blended family.

But after three years of marriage, the kids started acting out and I was losing ground with them.

"Ma'am, I have your son in custody," the officer said. "He hit a telephone pole on slippery roads and tested positive for alcohol." My heart pounded. "Because he's only 16, we can't keep him and you will need to pick him up."

My Life Falls Apart

Although I had talked face-to-face with him only hours before, Mark was arrested for DUI. He had begun to fill the holes in his heart from his childhood with drinking.

One evening I rushed home after work to get my stepdaughter to her choir concert. My sons told me someone had picked her up right after school.

"Tell mom I won't need a ride," she had said. I knew her real mom was going to attend this special concert.

When I arrived with the other kids, I scanned the choir, but could not find her. It was a large high school choir, so I asked the boys if they saw her. They shook their heads no. After the concert, we waited in the car for her. Seeing her across the parking lot, stumbling in her heels with her ripped slip hanging lower than her dress, my mind raced as to how I would explain this to her dad. She had shown up intoxicated and was suspended from school.

All four of the kids were not only smoking, but also smoking in the house, because "dad does it." I couldn't be there all the time to monitor them and now my beautiful new home was at risk of burn marks and walls smudged with smoke.

The kids were also talking in disrespect to me and the more I tried to maintain control, the more helpless and alone I felt. Being a strong but loving parent to teenagers seemed out of my reach. I felt inadequate and failing further damaged my self-esteem. I was so ashamed.

Tension in our home was building. It was "your kid did this" answered with "well, no different than what your kid did last week." Lee was finding more and more fault with his stepsons. They were using and losing his tools, disregarding curfew, and jumping out of their window during the night. I felt like he favored his kids, and I am sure he thought I favored mine. I was trying to balance my loyalty to my kids and my loyalty to my marriage. So although I was incredibly in love with my husband, I still carried the guilt of not protecting my sons from their father's abuse throughout their early lives, and now their new dad was starting to reject them too.

However, I never lost hope that the happy home I had dreamed about my whole life would evolve at any moment. From day one, I felt certain that Lee, my 'savior', who had delivered us from the jaws of hell, was part of God's plan for my sons and me. I trusted that plan with all my heart even when at times I felt it slipping through my fingers.

My life began to unravel.

Traded In For a Motorcycle

Losing my income from the law firm financially devastated our family. The economy was bad, and jobs were few. Our living expenses were overwhelming on just one income. Lee had a budget, paid the bills and I respected him for handling an overwhelming job that kept us financially afloat.

One hundred resumes and two dozen interviews later, I was offered a new job. After six bleak months our family's future looked promising.

"Well, here it is," I said to Lee as I handed him my check. "My first paycheck in a long time."

Lee did the banking during the day since I was at work.

"See you tonight, honey," I said. "It's the weekend, and we can be together," I gave him a kiss and a hug, and rushed out the door for my commute to work.

Thank God, it was Friday. I was exhausted after a long workweek and driving home in heavy traffic. I walked into the house where all of the teenagers plus one were bouncing off the walls. My stepdaughter had brought a friend home to spend the night.

"Dad said he didn't care," she said. And I didn't care. One or more of the kids often had a friend over on a weekend night.

I strolled into my walk-in bedroom closet to hang up my jacket and stopped. My eyes scanned the entire closet as my mouth dropped open. What the heck? Nothing could have prepared me for what I saw.

Shame Shame Go Away!

My husband kept the closet perfect. He had one side, I had the other, and all of the hangers were hung the same way. His short-sleeved shirts were hung together, as well as his long-sleeved shirts.

But now, his half of the closet was empty. Where were Lee's clothes? Were they stolen? Running back into the bedroom, I checked the dresser for his underwear, socks, and folded tee shirts. Everything was gone. Was this a joke?

I ran to the desk where Lee kept all our financial budget records, checkbook and savings account book. Gone. Even the calendar where Lee methodically recorded when our bills were due was gone.

My legs weakened, then buckled, and I went down. Sitting on the floor, I pounded my fist into the carpet. How could this be? Where did he go?

When I kissed him goodbye that morning, he hadn't said anything about leaving, but he had moved out. We didn't have a fight. So why would he leave?

With every bit of voice I could muster, I yelled for the kids.

"Can you come in here a moment?" I stayed sitting on the floor as I tried to find the words to tell them dad was gone. He had left but not taken his children. They were still in the place where we had built our love nest – our beautiful new home.

The kids had many questions and I answered them as direct as I could, but I did not have answers.

"No, I don't know where he is."

"No, I don't know why he left."

"No, we didn't have an argument."

"Yes, his clothes are gone."

Traded In For a Motorcycle

"I'm sure something unplanned must have come up."

"Maybe this was a mistake."

I could not give an explanation because there wasn't any. I called him at work but he wasn't there.

I knew I had to maintain control so the kids would not panic, so I asked them to stay at the house all evening. I was going out to find him.

Trying to keep the car on the road while shaking all over, I drove to his sister's house. No one answered the door when I knocked; but parked in the driveway was a beautiful new motorcycle. Whose cycle was this? It wasn't something his sister would have purchased. I felt a hard lump in the middle of my stomach.

As I sat in her driveway, panic crept into my chest, choking me. What should I do? I knew I couldn't drive around much because I had limited gas, and very little money. After giving my husband my first back-to-work paycheck that morning, I had $9, and the kids needed milk for their cereal for the next morning.

I had no choice but to return home and wait for him to call. I felt like I was in a trance. When I returned to our house, the kids started up with their questions. It was then that my eyes filled with tears, and I cried my heart out. The kids comforted me and promised they would never leave.

Eventually the evening ended and I fell into bed with my clothes on and sobbed myself to sleep.

Morning came as usual. The world had not ended, but the end had come to my world.

I told myself that I had responsibilities and needed to remain calm. This was the day Lee and I were to serve as master and mistress of ceremonies at a wedding for the daughter of our best friends.

"Lee is so outgoing and personable," the bride had told me as she planned her wedding, "He's a natural master of ceremonies."

I had my role as mistress of ceremonies and Lee had his role. How was I going to pull this off?

With swollen eyes and no makeup, I dressed and went to the church. The plan was that I would help them prepare the sanctuary for the wedding and food for the reception.

I approached the bride and her mother.

"I have a big problem," I said. "Lee has left so I doubt he will show up this afternoon. I am so sorry." I started to sob, my legs gave way again and I landed on a heap on the floor. "I can't do my job either. I just can't."

Looking stunned, neither of them said a word. I pulled myself up, walked out the door, and drove back home.

Lee did not call me. After a couple of days, the kids realized he was not coming home and they were angry. But not at dad, at me.

"What did you do?"

"Will he get over it and return?"

They were full of questions and I did my best to answer them although I was filled with disbelief.

Within the first three days, I discovered that the motorcycle at his sister's house belonged to him. He had used all our money, before bills had been paid, including my first back-to-work paycheck as a down payment for the new motorcycle. After he left that morning, he bought the bike, and closed our joint accounts. He then prepared for a weekend trip with friends who

Traded In For a Motorcycle

also had motorcycles. Meanwhile I stayed home alone with the kids, and tried to figure out how I was going to feed them.

Nine dollars is not much to live on and it would be another 12 days before I would be paid again. I needed to swallow my pride and ask for money from my family. That was a very difficult telephone call to make and I hated dialing the number. I had believed he would return before I would need to tell them. I had planned to keep it a secret, so my family would never need to know that my perfect marriage and family wasn't so perfect.

I was humiliated, embarrassed, and ashamed but I needed money for gas and food. Of course, my family came through just as they had when I lost my job.

I continued to question myself. How could I have been wrong? Did I misjudge him? Wasn't he the wonderful person I thought he was? I had no reason not to believe him.

I often found myself in a trance, staring into space and seeing nothing. Sometimes I even did this when I was driving. I would find myself on a road, and wouldn't know how I had arrived there. I would be at a traffic light and remain stopped, even when the light turned green. I kept repeating: He left me. He left me. Why did he leave me?

When I finally talked with him, he said, "It wasn't working out. The kids fought and caused problems for us. It just wasn't going to work."

While the four children fought at times, they had blended into a family. They wanted us to stay together.

"I don't have any place for them right now, so can they stay there with you?" he said.

Shame Shame Go Away!

I knew that each child was dealing with this abandonment in different ways. They all loved him and blamed me. I even blamed myself. I didn't know what I had done wrong, but I believed it was my fault.

How long had he planned this move? Was he waiting until I was employed before he replaced me with a motorcycle? I felt so worthless. A motorcycle was more important than our marriage. The unconditional love I craved all my life was gone.

The mortgage payment on the house, pole barn, and 20 acres was more than I made in a month. The kids loved where they lived and did not want to move, however, I explained to them that we had to move as soon as possible.

I was fortunate to find a buyer for the home and property very quickly at a tremendously reduced price. I needed to dispose of the huge mortgage so I could afford food, gas and other necessities for the family. I found a much cheaper and very small house in the city and moved the family into it.

I made good money, but it took a lot to feed and clothe teenagers so I worked all the hours my employer could give me. One hundred percent of the time, I functioned both at my job and at home as a robot.

Lee rented an apartment in a few months and then moved into a woman's house with four kids who worshipped him just as my sons had trusted him with their hearts.

My self-image continued to deteriorate as every day I grieved and mourned the loss of my marriage. I had been so convinced that my marriage to Lee was part of God's plan. Broken hearted and hopeless, it totally encompassed my whole life, emotionally, spiritually, and physically.

The Effects of a Broken Heart

The failure of my second marriage played havoc with my health. I was diagnosed with fibro-cystic breast disease. My breasts would form cysts as fast as they were removed and sent to the laboratory. My surgeon reminded me that stress played into the formation of my cysts and he warned me to seek a stress-free life.

One of lab reports came back that the tissue was suspicious for malignancy. A lumpectomy, removing half of my right breast tissue was performed. The following year the other breast had a diseased cyst. The biopsy showed a large area on the side of my left breast that needed to be removed.

Just as the surgeon removed breast tissue piece by piece, my dream for a happy family life was dissected.

Once again, I hid from people that I knew were judging me as a divorcee times two. I hated the stigma of abandonment, yet I took all of the blame.

Days turned into months before I decided I was neither married nor single. I needed closure. I couldn't trust he would stay, even he wanted to return. I still loved Lee but realized sometimes love just wasn't enough. I knew I could never trust his love or commitment to me again. My ability to trust was gone. I filed and was granted a divorce.

While I longed for closure, it didn't come for many years. I continued to have dreams of Lee two to three times a week, and carried love for him for several years.

Shame Shame Go Away!

I wasn't the only one affected by Lee's abandonment. There were holes in my sons' hearts. They carried with them the scars of their abusive father, and the abandonment of their second dad to whom they had attached themselves. I believe they felt as unworthy as I did for a father's attention or approval.

Mark was continuing to drink and getting into legal trouble. Believing that I failed by being too lenient with Mark, I tightened the rules with Michael so he wouldn't follow in his brother's footsteps. He rebelled.

Michael was very attached to his former stepfather and stepsister. When I set my foot down after finding beer, I told him I could not deal with his drinking. He moved out and moved in with Lee who allowed Michael to drink in the home he shared with his new family. When Michael left at age 16, I was devastated and felt there was no end to my loss.

I sold the little house and moved into an apartment alone. How did I get here? I have no marriage, no family, no home, and I was living paycheck to paycheck in a shame-filled existence.

Within a few months, Michael and his former step-sister were moving into their own apartment. They were 17 and 18 years old, and expecting a baby.

My son and stepdaughter had suffered loss too. When Lee and I separated, they lost their second family. They were devoted to one another and to our family as our marriage disintegrated. Needing a family they became intimately involved and brought an innocent baby into the world. Lee and I would share a baby grandson and later, a granddaughter.

I was in a familiar place with feelings of loss, shame, and guilt. When I was down to nothing and nobody, I turned my life

The Effects of a Broken Heart

over to my Higher Power and I felt God's Spirit within. I had hope for a future if I could stay away from dating for a while.

Three Times Should Be a Charm

The last thing I needed was another man when along came James. Instead of taking the time to heal after a devastating divorce, I was honored with the attention James gave me.

James was a cute baby-faced man in the office building where I worked and was a player with all the women. I tried not to care when I saw him flirt with others, yet I felt really good when he wanted to be with me. I told him about my life and he seemed to listen. When I was through talking, he would say a few insightful words that made me believe he understood.

I did notice that he was often with other women, listening to them as well. He not only was trained to listen empathically but also had taught the same listening skills to volunteers for a helpline crisis answering service. He had perfected his style and women loved it. I was a prime example of a needy woman who responded to his empathy and he recognized it.

After my dream marriage with Lee had ended in divorce I had a distorted attitude about men and was known for giving other women advice on men.

"If there is anything resembling a red flag in a relationship," I would say, "Run." Too bad I ignored my own advice as I paid no attention to the red flag that was waving in front of my eyes.

James and I started dating, and too soon into the relationship, I stayed overnight at his apartment. While there, he made a phone call to a young woman he knew and would give him phone sex anytime he called. It turned him on to have sex with

Three Times Should Be a Charm

me while talking with this young girl. I wasn't comfortable and knew it wasn't healthy, but I didn't tell him I didn't want to participate. My body felt used and I wondered if this was what a prostitute felt. If only it had occurred to me that I deserved someone to make love to me and not to a fantasy. Hadn't I learned anything in my past marriages? Did I think I deserved to be treated this way?

For two years, first on, then off, we struggled in our unhealthy dating relationship. Most everything I did or said seemed to irritate him, especially the caretaking or nurturing part of me. He voiced his displeasure of who I truly was and in my usual manner, I started to change into who I thought he wanted me to be.

I was still grieving the loss of my marriage and the dream of a healthy blended family. My love for Lee still filled my heart and James was obsessed with the idea that I would see Lee behind his back. James would check up on me, just to see what I was doing or whom I was with. I knew so much about stalking yet I didn't recognize that his behavior was unhealthy. He always accused me of cheating on him and I fought for my right to be trusted.

We would terminate our relationship and both of us would grieve the loss. I was the needy one, but if I turned away from him and showed the strength to go on, he would panic and come crawling back. It was a tiresome game.

One moment I thought I loved him and then the next, I thought of how much I still loved Lee who had another family.

Abused, abandoned, and with two divorces, I was so desperate for love that I would do anything to find a respectable man who wanted me. At times I sensed that James thought of me as a leach that sucked the life out of him.

He wanted many women and envisioned them fighting over him. While we dated for two years, he would not commit to dating just me. Since we worked in the same building, I watched him flirt with every attractive woman. He flaunted how he dated others in front of me especially much younger women.

When I had an opportunity, I would date other guys. This was very upsetting to him.

"I can date others but that does not apply to you," he said.

We did promise to be intimate with only each other. However, while snooping at his apartment, I found a partial box of rubbers. When I questioned him about it, he was very good at putting me on the defensive and the missing prophylactics somehow became my fault.

One noon hour, as we ate lunch at Mr. Burger, he proposed to me. It was very unexpected and not in any way romantic. Later, he called it the biggest mistake of his life. In retrospect, I don't think he had given it much thought.

"If I'm not careful, I will lose you," he said. "I better grab you while I can."

He asked me to marry him before we even committed to just dating each other.

"Yes," I said.

Of course, I said yes. I could never ever say no, especially to anything a man asked me to do.

Now we were engaged. Caught up in the moment, I felt good. I wanted a committed relationship, but I wasn't sure I could trust another man enough to marry him. Yet, it was obvious I did not think I could live without a man in my life.

I thought James was a good catch. He was very handsome, had a great sense of humor, and seemed understanding of me.

Once James asked me to marry him I sensed he regretted it. He would often say he could not go back on a commitment and asking me to marry him was an obligation.

I insisted we remain engaged for a year before we were married. James agreed with me and later that evening he took me ring shopping to make it an official engagement.

During that year of engagement, James was diagnosed with depression and prescribed an anti-depressant. I could feel his resistance to get married. The fear of failing again kept me from being strong enough to say, 'Let's put us both out of our misery and cancel the wedding.'

With neither one of us looking at other options, we married. James had built a wall around himself and I thought a long engagement would give me a chance to break it down. His fortress kept my love out and denied him the ability to love me. I believed he had feelings for me, or did he?

When it was going good between us, we had a lot of fun. I had what I thought were true feelings of love for him. I would tell him I loved him, but he would answer me in a rather singsong voice, "Love you too." Every time my heart would feel warm towards him, I would tell him two or three times a day that I loved him, until he told me that I was telling him I loved him too much. After that, I always thought first before telling him. I felt restrained in expressing myself to him.

Shame Shame Go Away!

James continued to withdraw and I could not bear to face another abandonment. I would adjust to whatever made him happy. I would win him over so we could have a wonderful life together. It was always about him as I tried to figure out how to please him. Yet every day I felt like a failure.

Meanwhile I was still convinced that if we put God first in our marriage we could overcome any dysfunctional issue. I promoted the habit of praying together at every meal and James obliged.

My next goal was to convince James that our marriage would be blessed if we went to church together. I quoted statistics of couples who were mutually involved in religious services. James had no background with regular church involvement so this was a whole new experience for him.

"Every week? You want to go to church every Sunday?" he asked.

We agreed that he would attend church with me three Sundays a month. I was pleased that he was willing to attend church with me at all.

My body had taken a severe beating. The toll from stress had resulted in over 40 breast biopsies. The two lumpectomies six years before did not keep the disease away. It became necessary for me to have a bi-lateral mastectomy.

My surgeon explained to James what this would mean in our three-year marriage as far as the surgery, the recovery, and the affirmation he would need to give me that I was still a woman.

This surgery defined my life in a big way. Although I had reconstruction, I felt very deformed. Afraid that James would not want me, I bought sexy bed attire to cover the huge scars, but my

Three Times Should Be a Charm

husband did not want to look at me naked. He was not interested in experimenting with my new body and resented the way I pushed him into having sex when it was not comfortable for him.

"I know you need this, but I just can't do it," he said.

From the beginning of our relationship, our intimacy had always been based on my husband's fantasy, not reality. I felt like a receptacle not an intimate partner. After my bilateral mastectomy, we lived together as brother and sister rather than husband and wife.

James was respected in the church we attended where he used his skills of public speaking and filled leadership positions with ease. I felt pride in the important role he played and encouraged him to continue to be active in the church. It also took the emphasis off our dysfunctional marriage and provided activities that gave him confidence.

"I think I want to go into the ministry," James said after a district leadership meeting. "I want to become a local church pastor. I heard the district superintendent talk about it today and it sounds good to me."

He went on to tell me that he would need to quit his job and go to seminary to become a licensed pastor.

A few years earlier when we were married, I thought I wouldn't have to worry about money. I believed that after numerous difficult years of supporting the kids single handedly, life would be much easier with my new husband's generous income.

Now James was telling me he was going to leave his job in an upper middle class position with benefits, and I would become the primary wage earner.

What had I done? I just wanted him to attend church with me. Carrying more than my share of the financial load would change my life.

The words from my mother when I was younger came back, "Maybe you should marry a minister, and then you can live in church."

A Life Change

Together James and I embraced a new life. He began his seminary education where he blossomed into a biblically educated pastor. While attending school, James served as the pastor of two small churches while I worked full-time and was thrilled to be the pastor's wife. On the outside, we looked like the perfect second career couple and we played our roles very well.

Like a sponge in water, James absorbed his Bible studies, and became an excellent speaker during worship and teacher of numerous classes. I wanted to be part of his ministry, and devoted every spare minute to making him appear to be the best pastor possible. I reminded him of events in the lives of his church members. I gave him suggestions for the children's sermon, and wrote plays for the youth group to present in church. The church placed him on a pedestal and I was proud of him.

However, James was an arrogant man who would never admit he was wrong or someone else was right. His belligerent nature wormed its way into his role as administrative officer.

"I heard the women's group talking about you after church today," I said as I tried to give him hints about what was being said behind his back. He ignored signs of trouble brewing among the leadership of the church but I knew how powerful certain people were and had seen how gossip could cause havoc in the life of the church.

Shame Shame Go Away!

"We need to love the unlovable, James. It's the way God expects us to be," I told him. James resented anything said in a negative way and did not heed my advice. He accused me of controlling his ministry.

Was it all about James? How he could use the church for his best advantage? Was this a popularity contest or a call to bring the good news of Jesus Christ?

Still I defended him to others and remained committed to him and his ministry. I gave him praise, affection and my actions both in public and private were based on my love for him. I was the pastor's supportive wife one hundred percentage of the time.

For many months, I felt as if the Spirit of God was telling me to explore a ministry. At that time, I believed it was a ministry for victims of domestic violence. Convinced by my husband that I possessed the God-given gifts to become a pastor, I decided to consider becoming a licensed minister.

"I hear the voice of God saying that you should have your own ministry," James said. "It's God's will for you." I believed anything James told me.

Being called into the ministry was a huge step for me. My conservative background did not even allow women to vote on church matters so exploring ministry had never been an option.

As I applied for denominational approval to begin the journey toward pastoral ministry, affirmation was given me by the higher church administration. I resigned from my financially secure employment as I began the process of attending seminary.

"Oh, Annie, I don't think this will work for you," my mother said. "You were never good at tests."

A Life Change

Nevertheless, I passed all the tests, and was well on my way to beginning my seminary education.

It was obvious James was not interested in what was happening in my seminary training or my student pastor position in a nearby city. When I asked him to attend a special event at the church I was serving, he was full of excuses. If I inquired about the activities in his church, he put me on the defensive as if I was being noisy.

It was obvious James did not want me to know what was happening in his church and that filled me with questions. Why was he trying to deceive me? Did he want more attention from women? Was it easier for him if I was out of the way?

Skilled in false empathy, his compassionate nature attracted women in need, especially young women. He had a kind listening ear. Just like he had enticed me, he was a magnet to women who were lonely. This was the trait that drew me to him and now he never gave me the time of day. It was as if he had moved on to other quests in his life.

His church was having an ice cream social and entertainment in the neighborhood park. "What can I do to help?" I said when I showed up.

"Dip ice cream," he said. While I was dipping ice cream, I looked out at the crowd, and saw him greeting visitors with a young woman from his church by his side. I felt replaced.

I asked him why she was in that role and I was not.

"You are so insecure," he said. "Why are you jealous of her? You have your own ministry."

When I began the ministry journey, I misunderstood James. He implied we would pursue a team ministry but that was not what he had in mind. My dream was for James and me to be in church ministry together. I believed that we would be a great ministry team as we both had specific skills to offer. Now I felt as though he had deceived me. I was disappointed that we would have two separate ministries.

I thought James believed in me, but he had lied to me for his own advantage and I was crushed.

Serving as a student pastor in a neighboring town, I decided to drive home to have dinner with James before a special service.

I came up to an intersection on a five-lane road when the light turned yellow; however, I was too close to the intersection to stop. As I entered the intersection, I noticed an approaching school bus making a left turn. What was she doing? Wasn't she going to stop? Didn't she see me?

As I proceeded through the yellow light, the oncoming bus turned into my door with such force that it pushed my car sideways. My vehicle went over a telephone pole guide wire and rolled over and over. At last the car landed on its roof and surprisingly, I was alive.

I felt angel arms embrace me, protecting and holding me in place. I was not only alive but conscious and as I hung upside down in my car I was shocked that my life wasn't over.

People rushed to help but my body was wedged between the roof and the seat. Blood dripped from the left side of my face into my eyes.

"God in heaven, help me," I cried out.

A hand came in the side window, took mine and I was no longer afraid. A man's voice spoke to me from where the windshield had been.

A Life Change

"Where is the other person who was with you in the car?"
"I'm alone" I said.
"But I saw another person."
"No, no, just help me."
"The rescue is on its way."
I had no doubt of whom he saw or whose arms were around me.

The Jaws of Life cut me out and the EMS rushed me to the hospital. Taken into surgery, a plastic surgeon put the left side of my face back together, fusing muscle and symmetrically rearranging my face.

My life changed on that day. Before the accident, I had chosen this epitaph for my tombstone: "Life is a bitch and then you die." But no more.

"Life is a gift," became my motto. I was so grateful that my life was spared and felt positive knowing that God had a reason and purpose for my life.

My face was disfigured since I had lost muscle and skin and it took months for the muscles to adhere and function in the proper manner. My mouth was crooked, and my pronunciation made it difficult to understand my words. After ample time to recover, I continued to prepare for full time ministry in spite of a debilitating setback.

A Church of My Own

It was after years of seminary and a near-death experience that the phone call came.

"I have a church for you," the district superintendent said. "It is in another county, district and area."

"What about James'?" I asked. I was concerned how this would affect him.

"In order for you to start your career, James will need to move to another church," he said. "He will receive a call in a few minutes from his superintendent."

My mind raced as I sorted out what I had been told. In order for me to begin my ministry in the church appointed to me, James would need to move to the other side of the state with me. This would mean that if we were to live together as husband and wife, James would need to be appointed to another ministry near the town where my church was located. James would need to sacrifice his church location for me.

James was angry, resentful, and depressed. This was not part of his plan for his life. He was used to having things go his way with the focus on him. He did not want to leave his 'king of the mountain' church and community.

He was accustomed to spending most of his days in the beauty shop/tanning booth in his small village. There he entertained the women of the community who were awed by his knowledge and handsome appearance.

A Church of My Own

Now James had to say good-bye to his first church appointment where most people loved him. He had had enough support by those who befriended him to keep the clergy killers at bay.

Hours away and miles from anything, James was appointed to a church with parishioners who did not worship him like a god. James hated the location and the people. In his resentment, he seemed to do everything he could to be what they did not want in a pastor. He argued and fought his way through three years of ministry with this congregation. His superiors suggested he needed to re-evaluate his ministry as it was not a popularity contest but it was a call to serve the church.

Answering God's call, we understood the denominational leaders determined where we were needed. It would be in that location where we would move and serve. We were not in control of where we were sent. It was a challenge for James not to determine the where, why, or what of his life. Every church had difficult members who were not supportive of the pastors they were sent. This was especially true in the case for James. He was forced to sacrifice his need for the power and popularity that he experienced in his first church appointment.

Feeling blessed, I started to grow in my profession as a pastor. This was the first time in my professional history that I felt as though my life had purpose. I loved the ministry, and the church congregation loved me. I spent 12 hours a day seven days a week being the very best pastor God empowered me to be.

This resulted in a promotion to another church in another city but there wasn't a church in that city for James to serve. He had to remain behind in the town where he had never wanted to go and hated in the first place. It was a very difficult time for him. We lived in separate homes in towns that were an hour apart.

"Behave, be loving and considerate of your church members; don't cause issues that divide the church; do not take advantage of the church; do your job as a pastor, or else!" This was the warning from the church administrators when they moved James the following year to a church location in closer proximity to my church.

Although our marriage was dysfunctional, this was a tremendous time for me with a successful ministry, a beautiful new church home, and another opportunity for James to pastor in a nearby church. I begged him to go to a marriage counselor with me. He wanted absolutely no part of marital counseling.

James had insomnia and roamed around the house at night. He would sleep on the couch, chair, another bed or anywhere except with me. He resisted the closeness of sleeping together, even though we were not having sexual relations.

I suggested to him that we purchase a $3,000.00 adjustable bed that could fit in the same bedroom next to mine. I thought that if he had a comfortable bed, maybe he would sleep in the same room with me. He agreed. Our marital bed was a queen and his adjustable bed was full size so it looked like a mile of bed placed together. It felt like we were miles apart in many ways.

After this investment I bought two bed spreads and sewed them together to look like one and pushed the beds together. I would reach across my bed in hopes he would reach out to me with his hand. Many times when I would reach out to him I would find that he had left the bedroom. I wanted a real live

A Church of My Own

body next to me. I continued to feel lonely without the affection and warmth of a loving touch.

While I was serving as a pastor, I attended further education for two weeks at a seminary in another state. At the college I met a man in my ministry class who was sweet and kind. We had many conversations where he affirmed my preaching skills, and complimented me on being attractive. In his life, he was lonely and empty as well. Although I knew it violated my marriage covenant, we became emotionally attached to each other. This happened at the end of our classes together. Although we stole kisses and embraces, we did not engage in sexual intimacy.

Our class ended and we returned to our individual home churches over 900 miles apart. We continued to email one another every day and talked on the phone several times a week. We shared the events of our lives and our ideas for ministry. We listened and encouraged each other. After feeling romantically dead for so long, my emotions felt alive again. This man was interested in my ministry and me and I was interested in him and his ministry. Although we dreamt of a time we could be together, both of us knew it was only a fantasy.

James and I had separate computers in our church offices. I never touched his, and he never touched mine. He was very computer savvy and had connections to companies that could help him find answers on how to fix or find whatever he needed.

During this time my son suffered an injury in another town, so I went to visit him in the hospital. James used this opportunity to gain access to my church office and spent hours on my computer, experimenting with passwords until he found the correct one. Checking my emails he printed off all the emails my male friend and I had shared. He then met with an attorney the following day to inquire about a divorce. Afterwards he came home to tell me about his discovery.

He told me that I was so lighthearted and giddy when I returned from my class that he suspected something had happened while I was gone. I believe he viewed it as an excuse to terminate our marriage.

I admitted my emotional affair and the fact that we never had sexual relations. Both my male friend and I were committed to our ministries and had no intention of ever getting together as a couple let alone ever seeing each other again. We lived on opposite ends of the country.

I begged James for his forgiveness. Without hesitation, I called my male friend and told him I could no longer have any communication with him, no emails or phone calls. He agreed with me. My heart really wanted to work on my marriage. I promised James I would never do anything like that again and I would never become emotionally attached to anyone but him.

What I did not fully understand was that James was not capable of loving anyone but himself.

My husband repeatedly reminded me of my emotional infidelity with my colleague.

"I'm sorry. Please forgive me," I asked on countless occasions.

He was not willing to grant me forgiveness or work on our marriage in couple therapy. I knew the marriage was never healthy from the beginning and now even less likely to develop into anything that resembled a normal marriage. I lived in a shameful existence for having caused him so much pain and wished I could undo the harm I had done.

"Just one phone call to your superintendent," he said, "and your ministry will be over."

I knew James could have me removed from my ministry. He had the proof that I had been emotionally unfaithful and held it over my head for the next seven years. He did everything he could to be repulsive and destructive to my ministry.

Of course, whenever he brought it up, I gave in to whatever he wanted. I was willing to do anything to keep him happy and quiet. My emotional infidelity continued to cause me shame. James controlled me as his prisoner and the anxiety dictated my life.

Even after all of this, I still loved James and wanted a future with him. I intended to spend the rest of my life with him. We had faced many trials together and I did not want to lose this marriage. Dysfunctional as it was, I did not want to be alone.

In my heart and soul, God gave me reassurance that I had been forgiven and continued to bless my ministry.

It seemed like the more successful I became, the more James resented everything about me and my ministry. He would tell people in my presence, "Everyone loves her," and then he would stick his finger down his throat, as if to gag himself.

A couple years after appointing him to his new ministry, and several run-ins with church leaders, it was determined that James could not function successfully as a pastor in his church. He never revealed to me the truth of what the accusations were against him but he was discharged from his duties as a pastor and his career was over. I did not know how destructive an angry man could be who does not believe he is accountable to anyone.

I lived with the fear that my colleagues and my church members might hear some rumors of why my husband was no longer able to pastor any church.

Although I was bonded to my ministry, we decided to leave the area. If we could leave this town, the loss of his ministry and the reminder of my emotional unfaithfulness might be left behind. Perhaps we could have a new start and there would be hope for our marriage.

My sister had died, and I was made the guardian of her mentally challenged daughter. I asked for a move to a church appointment in a town by her adult foster care home and near my elderly widowed mother. I was approved for a new ministry on the other side of the state.

Touring my beautiful new church for the first time, I watched as James longingly scanned the building. I sensed that he was wondering why I should get this opportunity and not him.

Another Church - Another Chance

Introducing my husband to my new church, I bragged about his pastoral and preaching skills. I thought that if I could make him feel important, needed, and a part of my ministry, he would feel better about himself. Instead, his anger towards me grew and he resented anything I said or did.

He walked out of the worship services I was leading and since he sat in the front of the church, it made a scene. When I returned home, I asked him why he walked out in the middle of my service.

"I was tired of listening. Sick of being there," he said. Therefore, whenever he had enough, he just stood up, walked out and went home. Others would stare at him or shrug their shoulders.

When his career as a pastor ended, it was still several years before James would be eligible for Social Security. He applied for numerous jobs but as a terminated pastor, he had no references. James was eliminated from the pool of candidates. If he was hired anywhere, the employment was short lived.

So James and I were dependent upon my church to provide us with a home and paid utilities. He had an expense-free place to live with me. Later, I realized he wanted the marriage to end but could not afford to live on his own. He also knew how another divorce would affect my ministry. With reluctance, he stayed with me and his actions every day made it clear how resentful he was.

Even in his previous occupation, before the ministry, James had a personality that focused on revenge. So it came natural for him to want to get even with those who he believed had ruined his vocation as a pastor. He took out this need to retaliate on me. Trying to be supportive and encouraging, I did everything to support him except leave my position as pastor of the church. At this time in my life, I knew if I resigned from my pastorate, it would be impossible for me to secure employment in any other profession. We both needed my income to survive. The stress wreaked havoc on me.

"Dozens of ulcers inside and outside of your stomach," the surgeon said. The ulcers had eaten a hole through my diaphragm and part of my stomach protruded into my chest cavity. I could have only clear liquids for the weeks before I had major surgery and the months following as I recovered.

Relegating authority to my husband while I recovered for six weeks, I was grateful he was available to help. It gave me an opportunity to give him praise as the church endeared him for helping while their pastor was on sick leave.

Staying on my feet had become a challenge for several years. I had this habit of falling; downstairs, upstairs, or walking on the sidewalk. I could be walking along and stepping on a pebble would cause my entire body to fall to the ground. I was off balance, and would bump into doorways, or drop things with no apparent reason. At times, my legs would be so weak I would have problems walking back home from the church next door. Numbness in my left leg would tend to make my foot drag and stumble. I was having problems thinking of the right word to use in a sentence either while serving in the pulpit or in my personal life.

Another Church - Another Chance

After many tests over five years, I was diagnosed with a subtle form of multiple sclerosis. It was the type of MS referred to as R & R – relapsing and remitting MS. The symptoms would come and go, sometimes lasting a short time and other relapses over an extended timeframe. The doctor stated the disease would move into a secondary progressive phase of inflammation in 20 years after onset.

Learning of my new diagnosis, I became heartsick and worried about who would help me as the disease progressed. James would not be able to help if it meant being intimately involved with my naked body. He was embarrassed if he caught a glimpse of me without clothes. How would he be capable of taking care of me especially bathing or inserting a catheter?

Shortly after this diagnosis, I received an email from a mother in my church who informed me that an email sent out to the church youth group for an upcoming event came attached with a page of pornography. I talked to the mother about it and called it a fluke.

I questioned James as to how this might have happened.

"Not anything I did," he said.

I believed him. Later I opened a credit card bill in his name and found he had joined an online dating service called Adult Friend Finders. I could not believe he would belong to an organization that would put my ministry in jeopardy.

I was paralyzed with fear that my church would discover that my husband, the pastor's spouse, was advertising for an adult friend. I was counseling others who had marital issues, and my own marriage was beyond dysfunctional. How could anyone understand that I, as a servant of God, had a message to bring them?

When I showed him what I had found, he did not deny having placed the advertisement.

"It's your fault," he said. "You did this."

I accepted the responsibility of my husband joining the Adult Friend Finders.

He started to stay at our retirement home an hour away more and more. I was asked often, "Where's your husband?" And I was embarrassed because I did not know how to answer them. Covering for James' absence, I decided it would be easier if I just requested another church appointment in closer proximity to where James was living.

Just before my move was announced, my MS symptoms became much worse. The stress of fearing another marital failure played havoc with the disease. Fatigue overwhelmed me and my eyesight became more blurry.

I fell walking from the church to the parsonage and injured my back. After several months of physical therapy, surgery was the only answer. As I recovered, I lived most of the time alone and felt abandoned.

Approved for a new church location, I packed, cleaned and arranged for the move from one town to the other. I was running again in fear that the truth of my marriage would be exposed.

Once again, my focus was on James instead of using my spiritual gifts to serve God in ministry. This was the biggest opportunity in my ministry and it was wasted. I was so ashamed.

Was there any hope for my future?

Is This As Low As It Gets?

After arriving in our new church home, my expectations were that James would fulfill his role as the pastor's spouse. I forced him to make his 'showing' and introduced him as my better half. I wanted him to be accepted but he glared at me as I spoke of his spiritual gifts. James had no interest in being there with me and hated every minute I forced him to spend with the congregation. Whenever I asked him to do anything, either for me personally or within the church, he would say, "Do me a favor, will ya? Just take a gun and shoot me."

Did I really think there was hope for a future as a pastor or in my marriage as long as I expected James to support my ministry?

Following worship one Sunday, James sat in the front row of the church and as I walked down the chancel steps, he said, "Why do you have a church? You don't deserve a church. I should have a church, not you." I was so humiliated and hoped no one heard him.

My pathology was that if a man said something about me, it was the truth. James said he should be the pastor, not me, so that was what my heart and soul believed. If I could, I would have given him my pastorate, but I couldn't so instead I felt like a failure as a pastor.

Some of my church members saw my husband's disinterest in my ministry and me as it became very difficult to even ask him to participate in the activities within the church.

Shame Shame Go Away!

"Where is your husband?" is a question I heard often. When the church members tried to be social and invite us over, he would refuse. The church family could see James did not like them, and did not want to become part of them. He was not going to participate in the role of the pastor's spouse.

Following the 'I should have a church, not you' incident, I asked him to sit in the back row when he did attend. When he had enough of the service, he could walk out without distraction. Yet to the church community, I continued to defend and support him, because deep in my heart, I loved him.

I also believed that the chance for me to be loved deeply, emotionally and physically was not attainable. There had to be something very wrong with me. I had been rejected and that meant I was unwanted and unlovable. On my 60th birthday, my heart was filled with sadness, yet no one knew about my sorrow, not my sons, my grandchildren, or my husband.

James was a master in designing web pages and computer programming. He designed a wonderful church web page and set up a graphic church newsletter. With both, I gave him ample praise both privately and publically. Eventually he used both to vent his rage at the church in articles he placed in the newsletter.

Once when my visiting teenage grandchildren were on my computer, I sat down at my husband's computer. As I wrote prayers for the service, the computer went blank and I lost the document I was working on. When I re-started the computer I went to the document index, looking for my file. It was then that I noticed a document entitled, If Only I Dared. I opened it and there was a lengthy description of what he thought of me, how he had no respect for my ministry, and how he loathed me. Included

Is This As Low As It Gets?

was a detailed description (if only he dared) of how he would murder certain people he thought had wronged him by 'dismembering their bodies.'

My blood ran like ice water through my veins. In his rage, was he capable of violence like this? How was his brain capable of forming such horrible thoughts? Now that I knew this, what should I do with the information? Threatening me with such words was one thing, but was some of these church leaders in danger? Ashamed to report this to anyone, I protected him by keeping quiet. If I said anything to him, he would think I was rummaging through his computer, and I had never touched his computer or anything in his files before. Even after finding such threats on the computer, I still felt I owed him respect.

For years I had worked with victims of domestic violence, and now I was questioning if he was capable of killing me or worse yet, someone else.

The latch on the back door of the parsonage was broken and the wind slammed it against the siding next to my bedroom window. One evening I jumped up in the middle of the night to close it. When I turned around, I was face to face with a gun.

"What are you doing" I asked. "You could have shot me."

Hearing the noise, James had grabbed his gun, came running and pointed it at me.

"I thought someone was breaking in," he said.

Facing that gun was a shock to me. Could he have shot me?

During this time, his online purchasing accelerated. I continued to support James as he continued to spend money. Numerous boats, motorcycles, off-road cycles, Detroit Lions clothing,

Shame Shame Go Away!

and antique baseball cards were some of the unnecessary items he purchased on the credit card.

I was concerned about overdue payments and overdrawn joint checking accounts. Yet I felt as though it was my responsibility to keep us financially afloat, and allowed him the freedom to spend as he chose.

His adult son, who was in poor health, lived in our small retirement home. James spent much of his time at that home with his son and his teenage grandson. When I visited, I was appalled at the filthy mess that had been made of my retirement home.

It was difficult for me, as a pastor to make friends. Often clergy couples have a social life with their church members, but this was not an option for me. As my husband spiraled out of control, I did not have a true friend with whom to confide. Then God placed a wonderful person in my life. Seeing how stressed I was with my personal life, this woman endeared herself to me and became helpful in a loving, supportive and nourishing way. Together we went to dinner and the theatre. She provided transportation for me on days when my MS symptoms left me weak.

In the past, I never believed that I deserved to have a good time, go places for mere enjoyment, or just laugh. Kris' unconditional love showered me with support and guidance as my personal and professional life spiraled out of control. She became the heart and hands of Christ during the dark night of my soul.

This woman and the unconditional love she gave me were wonderful. Kris genuinely cared for me.

One day over dinner, I told her how a few months earlier, I felt as though my life was doomed. I had planned to spend the

Is This As Low As It Gets?

next two years finishing my commitment to God with my ministry in the church and then I would retire with my dysfunctional husband and 'will' myself to death. I knew my marriage had no future and James and I had no similar interests to enjoy our retirement days. I anticipated that retirement would bring me no significant change towards happiness.

"In fact," I said, "As soon as my appointment within this church is complete, I wish I could promptly die."

She was shocked. I discussed with her my concern of who would take care of me when my MS disability caused me to lose more and more of my ability to function. I did not know what I would do or where I would go when I could no longer take care of myself. My husband would not be able to give me the care I would need.

Kris then promised that I would never need to worry. She wanted to take care of me or see to it that I would not be alone when I became disabled. She relieved my fears and was a gift sent to empower me.

Giving me confidence and reassurance that I would not be alone, she affirmed that I was a worthy and precious person who deserved to be unconditionally loved and not abandoned as my physical body deteriorated. Kris had given me hope.

Calling It Quits

"Have you taken a look recently at the church's web page?" a church member on the phone asked me.

"No, not recently," I answered.

"Well, you had better take a look," she responded.

Going online I could not believe what was on my church website for everyone to see. James was advertising a gun for sale. Included were a picture and a description of what the gun could do.

When the news of the website exploded through the congregation, I received a phone call from my district superintendent.

"Some of the members have said they won't be back to the church," said my superintendent. "His actions are viewed as a threat to their safety."

It was then I had to come clean and tell about the file entitled, If Only I Dared. While telling the superintendent the details of the file, I recalled an incident of more than six months before.

"What are you looking at," I had asked James as he looked out of a door facing the church.

"I could not knock them off from here very easily," he said, "and no one would know where it came from."

The members of the church were just leaving a meeting. His hatred toward specific people who had envisioned him for who he really was had been taken to another level. I had blown it off as James' insanity.

Calling It Quits

I did not want to face the facts. James was not stable and I could not risk my safety or the safety of the members of my present church and the administration of the denomination. I did not believe James would follow through on his threatening behavior but enough doubt necessitated taking a step to sever his relationship with all of us.

I asked him to leave the home. He could have what he always wanted and no longer needed to play the part of my spouse in or out of the church.

All of the many threats and blackmails to expose me had come to an end. The marriage was over.

If anyone ever would have told me in my 'perfect daughter/perfect wife' days, that I would have three divorces, I would have called that person a 'liar.'

My third divorce, terminating my longest marriage of 18 years, did not come easy. No matter how rejected, how unfulfilled, and how used I had been, I still cared very deeply for James.

Why did I continue to love a man who did not love me and never had my best interest in mind? I hung on to a lifeless marriage that James never wanted.

Throughout our marriage, James had admitted to me that he was capable of doing many crazy things. I knew he was jealous, resentful, and capable of retaliation when he didn't get what he wanted. He was depressed, but even more, he was mentally ill. He was sinister.

For all his empathy skills, he was not capable of feeling the pain of others. I never knew anyone who could hate as he did. He even hated in the name of love.

Shame Shame Go Away!

I just wanted to be loved.

Why couldn't he just love me? Was that so hard?

The finalization of the divorce wasn't the last interaction I had with my former husband.

Several months later, he stopped by to exchange boxes of leftover marriage memorabilia. He grabbed me and fondled me, forcing me to touch him. As I fought him, he overpowered and pushed himself into me. My insides felt like they were ripping apart. Just as fast as he arrived, he left. I cleaned off the blood, dressed, and went on with my day as if nothing had happened. I had been worried that he had something planned to get even with me since retaliation was his middle name, and I was right. I thought it was my fault so I didn't tell anyone. It was an act of power and control, fed by anger, resentment, and the need for the last act of degradation.

A couple weeks later, I was attending one of my numerous church meetings. Often during church committee meetings, I would be faced with difficult people and sometimes our conversations became rather contentious. I had faced such meetings numerous times in my pastoral career, and this meeting was no different.

Without warning, I became hysterical, screaming incoherently, as my body caved in, and I slouched onto the floor. I could not stop crying and did not have the strength to move for several minutes.

I had lost it emotionally and physically with no reasonable explanation as to what had happened to me. Somehow, my nervous system gave in and gave up. Weeks of exhaustion followed which forced me to take a leave of absence. During this time there were numerous church meetings which eventually led to my early retirement. A pastor of a church is someone the church needs to respect and I had lost it. Financial benefits were still six months away but my career as a pastor was over. I was no longer able to fulfill God's call to lead His church.

Loss of Identity

In the months following my exit from the church, I struggled for my place in life. Where could I go when I felt the church had chewed me up and spit me out?

When my marriage to James terminated, my shame and pain barricaded me from my loved ones. My heart split open when I wasted precious years of a relationship with them that I could not retrieve.

What I failed to realize was that my loved ones would not judge me because I was getting another divorce.

There was pain in every fiber of my being and I wanted nothing that reminded me of my failures. I wanted no reminders of my failed marriages, my ministry or financial losses, and the few leftover church friends from my various ministries. I even shut myself off from my kids and grandkids. I was judging myself and saw myself as a bad wife, bad mother, bad daughter, bad sister, bad aunt, and bad grandmother.

I gave everything I owned away with the exception of a few boxes of photos and mementoes of my childhood; my deceased parents and sister; my sons and grandchildren. I gave away my furniture, my cookware, my china, silverware, books, and most of my clothing. This included everything I had moved 14 times in those 45 years. After my sons took what they wanted, I called Goodwill Industries to take away the remainder of my life. I wanted none of it. The pain, shame and loss were so great that I

Loss of Identity

wanted no reminders of any of it. I wanted to deny my life happened because I blamed myself for failing.

Finances were limited because I was still months away from Social Security and retirement benefits. Wanting to earn my own way, I looked for employment. I applied for every position in the newspaper and online that met my qualifications. Since my worth as a human being was based on using my empathy and spiritual leadership, my heart was filled with the overwhelming sadness that I could no longer be a useful tool to individuals who could benefit from the skills God had given me. Feeling worthless continued to plague my life as I struggled to be emotionally stable. Finally, I gave up on pursuing a new professional life.

My dear loving friend, Kris, gave me a place to live in her home. She was the one person I trusted. She generously supported me, and I lived with her for a year. Her home became mine as I began a long journey of healing.

During this year another major stomach surgery was necessary. Kris lovingly nursed me back to physical health.

Kris' house was in the community where I served my final pastorate. The risk of running into people from this church community, at the grocery store, the post office or the doctor, gave me anxiety. It reminded me of the days when I was going through my first divorce, and I was hiding from anyone in the conservative community who had judged me to hell. I also cut myself off from my pastoral colleagues. I was so ashamed of how I had 'retired' from the church, avoiding questions, dirty looks and insinuations.

Shame Shame Go Away!

When I lost my position as a pastor, I lost my identity and I believed my life was over. How sad that my pastoral career had ended in such a despicable way!

All of the shame I carried for so many years, the parts of my life I kept hid, and all of the heartache and loss had crept up on me. I was as broken as Humpty Dumpty who fell off the wall.

Could anything put me back together again?

Grieving Loss of Family

My family of origin was plagued by disease and accidental tragedies.

Surviving a cerebral hemorrhage and a lifetime of alcoholism, my father died at age 60 from cancer. As he lay dying, each one of us told him we loved him. Our parents had never been in the habit of speaking the words "I love you" to each other or their daughters, nor did we reciprocate them back to them.

"I love you too," he responded in his slurred drugged state to everyone except me. I said the words over and over to him, desperate to hear them repeated to me. But my dad died without ever telling me he loved me.

All three of us as sisters worked together trying to contain our mother's erratic and manipulative behavior. Both Margaret and Joanne were more expressive in their approach of dealing with mother.

Still seeking Mother's approval, I continued to appease her by trying to be all she wanted me to be, yet realizing I would never be good enough. When my sisters would hurt her with words, I tried to remain the kind, soft, good daughter. Although I was constantly criticized from early childhood until the day she died, I was the daughter, according to mother, who most resembled her physically, emotionally and spiritually. For years, I struggled with believing this was a compliment.

Margaret's husband died in a tragic automobile accident at the age of 40 and our sisterhood deepened after the tragedy. The three of us vacationed together to the Bahamas, Las Vegas, throughout Michigan and the surrounding states. Often I felt obliged to Margaret because she came to my financial aid on many occasions. She was a very powerful force in our family.

Sometimes I felt like I was the sister on the outside of the family circle, because Margaret and Joanne resembled my father's side of the family and possessed many similar physical attributes. My sister, Margaret, was less critical of Joanne than she was of me. Many times her controlling nature frightened me into feeling, doing, and being what I did not want. This was so difficult because so many people controlled my life often at the same time: husband, mother, and sister. Trying to please everyone was a tiresome, all-consuming part of my life to the point that I had no sense of self.

My family had this habit of exaggerating the truth both outside and inside the confines of our family. Sometimes I would question who we were trying to impress and why it was necessary. This was especially true of my mother and Margaret. Both of them would speak to me about the other and it made me feel sad.

My younger sister, Joanne, and I had a loving, supportive, nurturing rapport all of our lives.

"I am crushed that I did not protect you from his sick, perverted behavior," I said to her after exposing her to Andrew's sexual exploitation.

"He's an animal," she said. "You had no control over what he did. I never blamed you. Never."

We were honest with one another, often sharing similar life experiences of failed marriages, health crises, and a lifetime of struggles. Joanne loved me unconditionally. No matter what error in judgment I made, she would still support me. Joanne even moved to the community where I lived to be closer to me although it did not fit into the lifestyle to which she was comfortable.

She and I suffered from both acute and chronic episodes of depression. Many times she wanted to end her life and I made every effort to hold her head above water until a crisis of suicide watch subsided. I often wondered how I would survive if she succeeded.

We raised each other's children as my two sons and her mentally challenged daughter were born within the same two-year timeframe. My sons defended their special-needs cousin, who was often teased as they attended the same elementary and middle school. Joanne was non-judgmental as I dealt with the acting-out scenarios and legal issues that began during my sons' teenage years.

Our relationship started to change as she became mean, cruel, and made derogatory comments to me when she began to abuse alcohol. I started to withdraw from her. As we continued to see each other at family gatherings, I no longer recognized my dear, loving sister. Losing my best friend brought me tremendous sadness. My heart was crushed.

Shortly thereafter, Joanne became seriously ill. As her condition worsened, she apologized and we reconciled.

During the months when she was critically ill, I filed legal papers on behalf of my sister for her mentally challenged daughter. We placed her daughter, my niece, into an adult foster care home. I promised my sister I would never abandon her only daughter and it is a promise I have kept to this day. She will always be like my daughter. My commitment at that reconciliation has never wavered.

Joanne's spirit transitioned to everlasting life when in my presence, she drew her last breath eight months later. Along with tremendous grief and loss of my best friend and sister, Joanne, guilt consumed me again.

As her physical condition weakened, I held the oxygen up to her nostrils for hours. Then early morning after a night of fatigue, I dozed off and dropped the oxygen tube. Joanne stopped breathing. I begged her to take another breath, but she did not. I felt like a failure, and thought it proved that I could not do anything right. I was a bad wife, bad mother, and now bad sister.

Lonely

For months following my sister's death, I would cry so loud in the shower that I would put a washcloth in my mouth to muffle the sobs. Lying on my back in my bed with a cloth covering my face, my tears would flow down into my ears. It was then that I believed no one would ever replace the relationship I had with my sister, Joanne.

For years afterwards, I would travel once or twice a week 70 miles away from where I was serving as a pastor, to spend the day with my mother, Joanne's daughter, and my sister, Margaret. Often the tension between mother and Margaret ran very high. When mother asked me to promise her that someday I would take my niece, out of the Adult Foster Care Home, and into my home, I did not hesitate to say, "Yes, I promise I will, mom." I took my only day off each week and traveled to be with my family on the other side of the state.

After I had moved closer to my mother, one Saturday, my niece called me and said, "Where's grandma? I called her yesterday and this morning and she hasn't answered."

Jumping into the car and driving 15 miles to her apartment, I noticed that her drapes were pulled shut in the middle of the afternoon. I knew then what I would find. My mother had been dead for 36 hours and seeing her body was an unimaginable shock. As my legs collapsed, I pounded the floor, with shouts of "No, No, No." I knew it was too late. She would never be capable of giving me the unconditional acceptance I needed. I would never be good enough. I was a bad wife, bad mother, bad sister, and now, bad daughter.

On the last day of my mother's life, my sister, my niece and I went to the department store she loved. My sister had lost her temper with mom, and I was angry that this was my very last memory of her. I was still married to James and looked to him for support, as I did with the loss of my sister, four years earlier, but to no avail. He was not capable of feeling empathy for the loss I was experiencing.

The time came when I realized that mother did the best she knew how to raise her daughters. She had her own issues with insecurity of who she was as a person; vacillating between inferiority and superiority. Without therapy, she was emotionally unstable all of her life. This did not stop me from loving her with all my heart.

Eventually I took my niece out of the AFC home, and into my own home. For nine months, I tried to make a comfortable home for her. However, I was not as firm as I needed to be and failed to give her the life she needed. Eventually I put her back into another AFC home. The one thing I thought I might be successful at to earn my mother's approval even after her death, I failed to do: bad wife, bad mother, bad sister, bad daughter, and now, bad aunt.

I continue to talk with my niece everyday and provide nurture and support for her in my visits, and taking her on vacation. I do not do this for my mother's approval. I do this because she is my flesh and blood, and I love her. My sons, well into middle age, love her and will continue to look after her long after I have left this world.

Lonely

As I went through my last divorce and the end of my pastoral career, other than my dear friend, Kris, my sister, Margaret, was my only confidant. I continued to spend one day a week with her and my niece. Margaret had a very strong, controlling and opinionated personality, yet I enjoyed the days we spent together caring for our niece. Since she was the final member of my family of origin, I wanted her to be proud of my career even as it ended so abruptly.

Within a month following my early retirement, Margaret was diagnosed with cancer. I panicked because I had been down this cancer road twice before with my family, and knew how it ended. The reality was that I would be the final living member of my family. From that time on, overwhelming grief, sadness and loss penetrated my life. While my family was dysfunctional, I loved every one of them. No matter the number of losses I had, I could always depend on my family, and they could depend on me.

After Margaret's diagnosis and while living with Kris, I started to travel 40 miles to my sister's home several times a week. I accompanied her to every doctor appointment, blood test, CT scan, MRI, and any other medical procedure she endured. I never left her side throughout hospitalizations, surgeries, and every medical decision. Each time she was rushed back to the hospital 30 miles away when the toxins would reach her brain, and her behavior was unstable, I was there and never abandoned her. I loved my sister with every fiber of my being.

As her condition worsened, I moved to her hometown and rented a furnished efficiency. I went to her home every morning and every evening to care for her in her final months. I needed to take advantage of every moment we had. It was so strange

Shame Shame Go Away!

because all of my life I never dreamed I would get this close and this intimate with Margaret.

In her final months, we became inseparable friends. We discussed everything - personal issues, politics, national and local news. She no longer was controlling or judgmental towards me, but rather accepting, loving, and sacrificial. Every day she wanted to take me to a different restaurant and buy me lunch. She could eat very little, but she wanted us to have an opportunity to talk, share and love. And we did.

"I'll be all right," I told her, wanting her to believe I would be okay. But my heart was saying how am I going to make it without you?

Facing her inevitable death and loss was unbearable for me. One by one they had left me. I felt like an orphan to be the last living family member and the path of grief was very lonely.

Wanted: Somewhere to Belong

"No, no, no," was my response when a friend insisted I meet a widower named Ray. "I want nothing to do with any man."

As much as she insisted, I resisted.

I had rented an efficiency apartment in the town where my sister, Margaret, lived. Being close to her was convenient as her health and well-being pre-occupied my life.

Talking to my friend about my living accommodations, she said, "Ray has a duplex near there and will be traveling out of state for the winter months. Maybe you can rent it from him and save some money."

"What's his last name?" I asked.

She told me his name.

"You're kidding. I know Ray from 40 years ago."

Ray was not a stranger. We lived in the same community for many years and had similar church backgrounds. Why wouldn't I dare meet him for coffee and discuss renting his apartment?

Deciding it wouldn't do any harm I agreed to meet him and we talked over coffee. Although many years had passed, we knew several of the same people. We shared our lives with each other and almost immediately I felt as though I had known him forever.

We had several health issues and both lived with the same type of Multiple Sclerosis. Neither of us had ever believed anyone who didn't have the disease could understand the fatigue, numbness, and scare of facing the possibility of eventual total disability.

Day by day, our physical strength might allow us to get around, and yet other days, we were too weak to get out of bed. We were in agreement that life in a normal relationship would be very difficult.

As I faced grief, sadness and loss Ray appeared in my life with understanding.

As we talked, I learned that after a 41-year marriage, the only woman he had ever loved had died seven years previous from cancer. As her loving caretaker until she died in his arms, he told me no one could ever take the place of his wife. His life had held no meaning since her death, and he merely existed. His physical pain and the emotional pain of loneliness never ended, and most days he wished it were over.

Introducing Ray to my sister, she immediately appeared comfortable in his presence. As her illness necessitated many quick trips to the hospital, he was patient and helpful in getting her there, and waiting hours as medical personnel determined what the next step would be. Ray also helped me with her daily personal needs. It was as if he understood the cancer dying process, physically, emotionally, and spiritually. He also had experience with Hospice and gave us advice as to what had worked best for him. With my limited family, I welcomed his nurturing assistance and caring ways. There wasn't anything he wouldn't do for my sister, Margaret, and for me as well.

There were no candle light dinners, no movies or romantic experiences as Ray and I didn't really date. We had a loving friendship. He listened to me as I prepared to lose my final family member, and I listened to him as caring for my sister reminded him once again of the journey of his wife's death.

Wanted: Somewhere To Belong

Ray was an honest and sincere man. There was no arrogance, no anger, no baggage and no abusive behavior. His nature was kind and loving. There were no red flags of danger.

Although he had endured seven painful years of loneliness, Ray did not pursue a social life. His wife was the only woman he had dated and known intimately.

"I have nothing to offer another lady," he said. "Financially I live on disability. And my health is shot."

I also believed I had nothing to offer another relationship. Having given all my earthly possessions away, I had no home, no furniture, no savings account, and I lived financially month by month in a one room furnished apartment. I had ongoing medical conditions that demanded hundreds of dollars of medications each month. I also had three failed marriages that had left me less than stable. Dysfunction felt like my middle name. Who would be willing to take on a three-time loser?

"I'm old," Ray said during one of our moments together. "I don't have time to sit around and wait. Let's get married so we can enjoy life while we still have our health."

As shocked as I was by his words, mine were even more surprising.

"Yeah, we could do that."

"This way when one of us deteriorates further in our disease, we won't be alone."

A peace came over me knowing I would not be alone. Immediately it felt like this was part of God's plan and I was comforted knowing I would belong somewhere and to someone.

Shame Shame Go Away!

I knew Ray's health issues were further advanced than mine, so when he told my sister he wanted to take care of me, I said, "Who is going to take care of whom?"

Living together for convenience sake was not an option for Ray. It was important to him that he set an example for his grandchildren. So unexpected for both of us, as well as our family and friends, we were married privately just before my sister transitioned from this life to the next. Before she died, she shared with me how relieved she was that I would not be alone.

In her determination that she not die laying down, Margaret always sat up until it was time to go to bed.

"I'm tired," she said early one evening. "I think I will lie down now."

"Good idea. Just lie down and rest in peace," Ray said.

Margaret threw Ray a kiss and lay on the couch. Shortly thereafter, she lapsed into a coma and did not get up again. She went to the hospice house and three days later she passed away.

Just minutes before Margaret took her last breath, she was trying to say three words to me repeatedly. I could not make the words out, but when I said, I love you, she nodded her head. Moments later, her spirit transitioned to her everlasting life.

Ray and I had shared our individual dreams of traveling before our health would no longer allow us to do so. Neither of us would have been able to safely travel alone.

Following my sister's death, our shared dreams became actual plans that gave me the hope to look forward to travel. They also helped me cope with the adjustment without Margaret.

The fall after Ray and I were married we traveled to every place I had always wanted to go. We went to the Great Smokey

Wanted: Somewhere To Belong

Mountains, then Branson, Missouri, then Myrtle Beach and finally a Caribbean cruise. It was a great vacation.

After we returned home from our travels, my emotional stability began to waver. I appeared happy on the surface, but my heart was not at peace.

Facing Shame Head-On

"You're not happy, are you?" Ray asked me following the return from our extended vacation. I interpreted the sadness in his eyes to mean that even though he tried every day to fill my needs, I was still depressed and without joy. He had tried to cheer me up whenever he sensed my sadness.

I was speechless to name my sadness, but I knew it came from deep within.

I had walked the valley of the shadow of death with over 200 families in the churches where I served as their pastor. Following my sister's death, I read books on how to accept the loss of a loving family member, yet I did not anticipate how this loss would multiply the grief of my many previous losses; people, places, relationships, and professions.

Grief could no longer be swept under the rug. I had to face sadness, loss and the need to give myself the time and kindness to process my grief. For years, many people had abandoned me. It now became necessary for me to admit the self-abandonment I had imposed upon myself for all my life. I never gave myself comfort, nurturing, grace, mercy, and love at any time during the losses in my life.

Reminders of my losses were everywhere. It was painful for me to witness others with parents, sisters, and extended family. Every time I watched couples my age celebrate significant wedding anniversaries, I was reminded that all of my marriages had failed. The loss of my sister opened wounds I never pro-

Facing Shame Head-On

cessed because I never knew how to deal with the loss, sadness and grief that I could no longer ignore.

All of my life I looked for unconditional acceptance and love. I never felt good enough, and no matter how much I tried, I never quite made the grade. If I could just be the person others wanted me to be, I could prove I was worthy enough to experience it. I knew I was broken so I held on to every relationship or marriage I had as I tried to be a people-pleaser.

Anytime my ex-partners, relatives, or colleagues said or hinted that my intellectual capabilities, spiritual gifts, or physical attributes were in question, I immediately believed I was all bad. I was a bad daughter, bad sister, bad mother, bad wife, bad grandmother, bad friend, and bad pastor.

Abandonment, rejection, abuse, betrayal, guilt, worthlessness and loss —the re-runs never stopped. The feelings that were generated from these memories had been stuffed for so long and I felt powerless over the shame that filled my being. That shame affected my relationship with everyone. I covered up my actions even when I had done nothing wrong. It took so much energy to hide whatever I did just in case it was wrong. I felt hopeless and was not able to express my emotions.

So when Ray asked me why I was unhappy, I could not begin to tell him why I was so miserable.

Years earlier, when my third divorce was final, judgmental acquaintances had made hurting comments.

"You're not ever going to get married again, are you?"

"You sure are not lucky at marriage."

"Is your partner picker broken?"

Shame Shame Go Away!

Feeling obligated to respond to my failed marriages, I would feel the need to reassure them, "Oh, no. I would never pursue another relationship, let alone marriage."

I acknowledged my inability to trust another man. I believed I had made so many mistakes and was so emotionally damaged, it would be impossible to maintain any healthy relationship. My failures did not deserve happiness so I would sabotage any quest toward sharing my life.

Now I was presented with a dilemma. Those who knew me were shocked that I had married again since I was so adamant about never getting involved with anyone again. How would I introduce my fourth husband?

When I began my new marriage, instead of joy, I felt shame. I didn't know anyone else who had been married four times. How could I expect others to accept me in my fourth marriage when I could not do so myself? How would Ray's family and friends react when they found out the truth about me? I imagined they would ask him if he was out of his mind for marrying me.

Ray had been married once which ended in his spouse's death. Divorce did not exist in his family or in the marriages of his friends. We had decided we would not share with any of them that I had been married three previous times to spare him this embarrassment.

I was always afraid that someone would recognize me from one of my prior lives so sometimes I lied when asked questions or I just left out some of the details about my past. Not living the truth had affected my emotional and physical well-being and I lived with constant fear.

Facing Shame Head-On

I deplored the deception I had become and had feelings of low self worth. I felt like a fake. I was so tired of struggling. When would I face this toxic shame?

Winter Sunlight

Facing severe depression, I was hopeful that some Florida sunshine would be helpful. Packing for a winter in the south, I spent a day meeting with my friend, Kris. As a Christmas gift, she gave me several books written by and for women. Kris was confident they would provide me the spiritual guidance for my dark night of the soul.

"You will enjoy these books and won't be able to lay them down," Kris said.

Doubtful, I paged through one of them.

"Why? What does this author know about my life?" I said. "Her life isn't anything like mine. She's famous and rich."

"Don't be so certain. Just read them and see what I mean," Kris said. "No matter how broken you feel, promise me you will not hurt yourself." She realized the level of my despair.

"Okay, I promise."

On Christmas Day 2010, Ray and I started our 976-mile trip between Michigan and Florida. When we arrived at our destination, it was dark, cold, windy, and deserted. The efficiency apartment was freezing cold, and the bed felt as if I was lying on a cube of ice. It matched my emotional state of mind.

The first morning as I opened the drapes to the sun shining on the waters of the Gulf, I felt its warmth like the arms of God. Right then I made a commitment to spend time every day meditating, reading and praying. I made a decision to begin a journey toward mental and spiritual health and wholeness. I would not surrender to the personal demons that plagued me.

"Why are you spending so much time reading and meditating?" Ray asked.

In the past if I sensed I had let my husband down, I would immediately apologize and promise I would stop anything that would keep me from devoting myself one hundred percent to them. Or if I was questioned about my emotional state of mind, I would concede, "Nothing's wrong. Just a little tired." I would not try to explain my emptiness and my sadness. My priority was meeting the needs, wants or desires of my partners, not my own needs.

For the first time in any of my relationships, I was able to be honest and say what I was feeling. I told Ray that I needed to set aside hours each day to read, meditate, pray and write, as I sought release of shame, blame and pain. I explained how I hated myself, and could not forgive all the mistakes I had made.

"I am at a turning point in my life. I need release of my pain and sadness," I said. "I need to find peace for all the mistakes I have made."

"Do whatever you need," Ray said. "Take whatever time each day to find what you're looking for."

In contrast to my previous husbands, Ray listened and understood my commitment to follow the Spirit's leading as I struggled for peace and joy. He did everything to help me free up my time to do whatever made me happy.

In spite of my past, my instability, insecurity, post traumatic stress syndrome, distrust of men, chronic depression, and thoughts of suicide, Ray was a loving friend. Even though he didn't know how to handle such a complicated emotional state, he was patient, understanding and kind.

What happened within that first week was nothing short of a miracle.

The life of this one author, Iyanla VanZant, was not different than mine. She too had faced loss, abuse, anger and shame. 'I so resonate with this author's life,' I wrote in an email to Kris admitting she was right after all. For the second time in a few years, she had saved my life.

Kris' unconditional love had supported me through the end of my pastoral career and had provided me a home and kept me from drowning in a pool of sadness, loss and regret. All I could do for those two years was to survive each day.

And now although we were over 900 miles apart, with her determination and confidence in me, I was able to begin my journey of healing. Online Kris and I bantered back and forth with her pumping me full of God's love and my arguing about my unworthiness. We became spiritual partners via computer sharing our prayers and thoughts with each other on a daily basis. And change began to happen.

Reading every book written by Ms. Vanzant, I became convinced that if her spirit was healed and her life was filled with peace and joy, there was hope for me. I filled my days with reading, mediating on scripture and prayer.

'Stop looking for love,' a still voice spoke to my soul. 'All of your life you wanted to be unconditionally loved by someone else. You cannot accept love without first loving yourself.'

But how would I do this? This self love concept was a challenge. I was so unworthy of being loved by anyone and especially love toward myself.

Miraculously, I opened myself to accepting that the Divine lived within me. At least I could accept loving the Spirit within, couldn't I?

I decided to look at who I was inside and found a new lease on life.

With an improved positive attitude, I inquired about a course in 'Writing your Memoir' at Florida Community College. I wrestled with the confidence to follow through with the class, but I was intrigued.

Once I started, I found that expressing my feelings through writing brought me tremendous relief. I wrote letters to my deceased sisters who had been my best friends and to my parents. I wrote pseudo-letters to people I had hurt or who had hurt me. I expressed in writing how proud I was of my grandchildren.

Classmates shared writings with each other. A bond of trust and approval formed in this weekly class. I started to feel confident with my writing style and was encouraged to tell the story of my life.

For years I had talked about writing a story of my life, but then I would think about it, and know I would make my story just a story. I knew I could not be honest. It was too embarrassing, degrading, and risky.

Now something dead inside was awakened and I felt ready to share my life.

If the women authors whose stories I read gave me hope, perhaps I could give hope to others. I started to make plans for my memoir. Now I had a reason to get out of bed each day as I added writing to my daily regime of meditation, reading and prayer. My soul was no longer dead.

Guest authors who visited our class encouraged me to write. My feelings previously demeaned, ignored or threatened were validated. Claiming the freedom to express my feelings gave me power to look at who I was.

Ten weeks in Panama City Beach had changed my life. I was on a path to emotional and spiritual health and I had hope for peace in my future.

When I felt the empowerment of the loving Spirit inside me, I started to discipline myself daily to keep the shame, blame and pain away. It would be something I would need to empower myself on an ongoing basis.

I had lived a lot of life and learned many lessons. Who was with me through it all? Who did not abandon me? It was THE SPIRIT OF GOD. I would continue to look to the Spirit of God who lived within me. The Spirit would help me on my personal journey toward healing, self-forgiveness, and self-love. Hope filled me that I could be free from the darkness of shame, guilt and self doubt to a life of sunshine with confidence and competence, giving me peace and joy.

I no longer wondered Where are you, God?

Forgiveness

The Bible is filled with stories about a forgiving God who patiently leads his dear children along on their journeys. I am one of those children. My journey evolved into a similar experience not unlike the Hebrews who wandered in the wilderness 40 years.

In the book of Exodus, we read how the Hebrews complained to the LORD about their conditions as they wandered in the wilderness for 40 years before their descendents arrived at the Promised Land. They disobeyed God, sinned, and worshipped idols, along with other failures of their faith. Over and over again, they were forgiven, just in time to turn their backs on God again.

This has been my journey of faith. Sin - forgiveness, sin - forgiveness, sin - forgiveness. My inability to accept God's unconditional love kept me begging for forgiveness. I not only asked to be forgiven for my present sins, but over and over again, I confessed every sin I could ever remember until the day when I felt the Spirit speaking to my heart.

'Every time you beg for forgiveness of sins long forgotten, do you not believe my grace is sufficient to forgive you?'

From that time forward, I never again doubted the grace of God that is greater than every sin I committed in the past, in the present, and every sin I will commit in the future. A loving and faithful God will forgive. This is how deep, how wide, how expansive God's grace has been in my life.

Shame Shame Go Away!

God's grace and forgiveness is beyond our human comprehension. All we can do is to accept the amazing grace of a faithful God.

I could accept God's forgiveness but I could not forgive myself. Since my goal was to become emotionally healthy and to start my life over with a new sense of self, it was necessary for me to forgive myself. I had made poor choices as a mother and spouse as well as making poor financial decisions, and other negative life circumstances. Learning to forgive myself was one of the most difficult things for me to pursue.

Sometimes when I talked with others about my life with much regret, they would tell me that I had done the best I could with what I had. Or someone would tell me that I had few other choices. These kind remarks gave me little reprieve.

"You don't understand. I cannot forgive myself," I would tell them.

For many years, I believed that I had no control over my life. I had no choice and no power over decisions that were made, until I chose to seek change in my life. In addition to letting go of the shame I needed to forgive myself.

"God, I am sorry I failed my sons."

"God, I can't forgive myself."

"God, please help me forgive myself."

"God, please help me today to forgive myself."

Over and over again, day after day, I prayed that God would empower me to forgive myself. Then one day the Spirit spoke to my soul.

'God has forgiven you. Why do you place yourself higher than God, by not forgiving yourself? Let it go.'

Forgiveness

"I forgive myself for my mistakes, failures, and my sins toward others and God. I forgive myself for it all. I no longer carry the burden of shame," I said aloud repeatedly. I could not argue with the truth of the Spirit so I forgave myself. I acknowledged the Divine Spirit controls my life.

However, the habit of negativity was well engrained into my brain, heart, and soul. There were reminders on a daily basis. What would I do when that happened?

Would I pick up the guilt or let it lay?

One truth remained in my conscience: I refuse to return to the black pit of shame.

On my journey in life, for over 60 years, I believed I was powerless over my life. The pit of shame, guilt, and self-hate lured me and falling and living in the pit was my reality. At times, I walked around the pit, trying to avoid it. Other times, my awareness of the pit encouraged me to attempt to build a bridge over it.

Shame brought suffering and I would not settle for suffering any longer.

When something unforeseen happened and I started sliding down the hill into the pit, I became conscious of my thoughts and feelings. I would decide if those were to be negative or positive.

Since I was in control of me, I told myself, "I refuse to return there. I want to remain on the path of peace and joy." So I prayed.

'Spirit within me, remain in control of my thoughts and feelings today.'

Shame Shame Go Away!

I now believe the day will come of total acceptance. There will be no need for self-forgiveness. The cover will be placed on the pit and sealed. Until then, I will remain on the journey that has changed my life.

Wanting the Best for My Sons

As a victim of emotional, psychological, and physical abuse, survival has been a journey that has affected every relationship my entire life.

And although I wish my life could have been different, I wish even more the childhood lives of sons could have been different. Their adult lives have been plagued with unhappiness, disappointment, addiction; loss, helplessness, and hopelessness due to their childhoods of abuse. Because even though they both felt they were doing everything 'right,' their lives continued to wallow in a negative existence. It reminded me of the words from *Exodus 34:7 . . . the visiting of the sins of the Father upon the children.*

Throughout their adulthood, guilt consumed me each time they were in a crisis. I felt as though I owed it to them to be there emotionally, physically and financially. After all, I had abandoned them as children when they needed my protection.

In my heart, they always came first, but I had made poor choices that affected their lives. I filled my own needs by marrying unhealthy men and failed to give them a stable family. I did not instill in them a positive self image nor did I teach them a value system that included planning for their future. I was too pre-occupied with my life.

For every failure, I took on the responsibility of whatever happened in their lives. I have tried to make it up to them ever since, but have gone about it the wrong way. I now know that no

Shame Shame Go Away!

matter what I try to do, I cannot change their past to give them another chance in life.

From their childhood experiences I believe they do not think that unconditional love exists and they lack the joy life can bring. For that reason, in the last year, I have tried a different way of communicating with them.

I no longer 'beat' myself up every time I see the unhappiness in their lives, and I talk to them on a different level. I seek their feelings when they question experiences from their childhood.

"Why hasn't dad ever told me he loved me?" my son, Michael, has asked me numerous times.

In the past I would say "I'm sorry" but then tried to change the subject. My guilt for their childhood abuse blinded me from really listening to them.

"How does it feel in your heart that dad can never tell you that he loves you? Do you feel unlovable?" I asked.

And recently, my son Mark said, "Mom, why did dad hate and hit me so much?"

"It must have felt like he didn't care about how much his blows hurt you," I said to him.

This communication has opened the doors to a mature loving relationship between my sons and me.

I now understand that their issues can be resolved, but I cannot do it. They will need therapy to work through the abuse from their childhood.

I know that the freedom from shame and doubt is possible and the journey of true peace and joy gives hope. I found it is never too late for this healing and change in the direction of my life. I want the same for them.

However, the responsibility to find the professional help for change in their lives is up to them. My prayer is that they can be on the same journey as I am toward emotional health and wholeness.

The Joy of Grandchildren

"Let me tell you about my grandchildren."

Those are the words of a proud grandmother, and no one loves unconditionally as a grandmother loves her grandchildren.

"I have the very best grandchildren in the whole world," I tell this to anyone who listens because nothing has impacted my life with such significance as my grandchildren.

Presiding as the birthing coach, I was present at the birth of my first grandson and was the first to cradle him in my arms.

"You are the most beautiful baby I have ever seen," I said. And he was.

For over 17 years, at least twice a month he spent weekends at my home, and I loved every moment we bonded together.

My second grandson was born six months later and I was present at his birth as well. After he was born, I alternated weekends as I took care of each grandson. Around the age of 14 months, I began to take both of them the same weekends, as they were already accustomed to being together as best friends and cousins.

On Friday evenings, after working full time in another town, I would drive an hour each way to pick them up and return them on Sunday evenings. It made for busy weekends, but I cherished every moment.

Grandson number two was a bright child and appeared strong in his first months. However, when it came time for him to crawl or pull himself up, he lacked strength. His intelligence

The Joy of Grandchildren

was far beyond most his age, but he lacked balance and leg muscles. After seeking an evaluation from a local child neurologist, his mother and I pursued a specialist at the state medical college where they determined my 16-month-old grandson had a genetic infantile form of Muscular Dystrophy.

After his diagnosis, I prayed for a miracle, "Please God, give my grandson a normal life so he can walk and run and ride a bike. I will give my life for him."

I joined a statewide grandparent support group and grasped every bit of knowledge about the disease I could. I learned that one day a disease might be as far away as the moon from your life and the next day, it can become your life.

My grandsons continued to spend time with me and every weekend I looked forward to their visits. They loved the time we spent together and grandson number one would push the second grandson everywhere in his wheelchair. He slept on the fold out couch in the living room and my other grandson and I slept on the floor next to him. Together we would roll him so he could breathe more easily. The older one helped the younger in whatever way he could.

Every day he lives his life from a wheelchair, yet he lives it to the fullest. Throughout his life, he has touched more lives with his courage, his optimism and his faith in God than I did as a pastor. He is the bravest person I have ever known.

During one of my many bouts with severe depression, I walked into my grandson's bedroom as he lay in bed.

"Hugs, Grandma, Hugs. I have missed you." I dropped to my knees, took him into my arms and prayed.

Shame Shame Go Away!

"Forgive me, God. How can I give up, when he remains faithful to the life you have given him," I said.

Grandchild number three arrived three years later.

"The baby is in distress and they need to take her," my daughter-in-law said in a message she left on my work phone. I left my job 70 miles away and drove to the hospital. When I got there, my tiny baby granddaughter had arrived by c-section. She was two months early. For over 20 years, I had dreamed of a pink nursery and frilly dresses. Finally my life was blessed with a girl after two sons and two grandsons. However, this itty-bitty bundle had numerous health issues that plagued her well-being for the first few weeks of her life. Her heart, lungs, and kidneys struggled to finish developing. There were times they stopped functioning and emergency resuscitation was needed. She was baptized two days after her birth as the doctors questioned if all the vital organs could function.

I had never cared for such a tiny baby, but when she came home, I confidently fed her, bathed her, and listened for the heart monitor to sound that indicated medical intervention.

I spoiled this beautiful baby girl and it was not long before she realized she had grandma wrapped around her pinky. Whatever her little heart desired, I did my best to give her.

"Has anyone seen my granddaughter," I said from the pastor's pulpit. From infancy, my granddaughter had accompanied me to whatever church I was serving. She was a social butterfly and made friends with children in every church. While I would lead the service, she would choose where she would sit. Her behavior was perfect, but when she was bored, she changed seats,

The Joy of Grandchildren

pews, or areas. When I couldn't find her, I would ask who had her.

Then, along came grandchild number four.

As the technician moved the ultra-sound camera over my daughter-in-law's stomach, it became apparent what she saw was not normal.

"It's boy," she told us. This would be a second son for this family. There were added concerns since their first son was born with an infantile form of a genetic disease.

"Yeah, another boy, that's great," my son said.

The following day my daughter-in-law called me at the office, "The baby has a cleft pallet."

I had feared another diagnosis similar to their first-born, but this hit us all by surprised and I crumbled.

"Why God why?" I said.

Long before my daughter-in-law was pregnant again, I begged God that if they were to have a second baby, it would not be born with the degenerative disease of their first-born. Now my son and his wife would have challenges with their second child.

I retreated to my home and went to bed where I asked not to be disturbed while I conversed with God.

"Dear God: From my earliest days, you have been a vital part of my life," I prayed. "You have always existed for me. I have begged you for several years for healthy babies. I have even tried to bargain with you."

I sat for a minute, and then started again.

"I know you exist, but today I don't believe you exist for me. Please show me where you are."

Shame Shame Go Away!

For 24 hours I prayed these prayers to no end. I cried, begged, and surrendered.

Finally, an answer came. In my heart and soul, I was led to read this scripture: *God, you shaped me first inside, then out; you formed me in my mother's womb. Body and soul, I am marvelously made. You know me inside and out, you know every bone in my body; you know exactly how I was made, how I was sculpted from nothing into something. Psalm 139.13-15*

Where nature makes mistakes, God will give my grandson what he needs.

Although his special needs demanded numerous surgeries, he grew physically, emotionally, and spiritually into a wonderful young man. He was born with determination and strength.

Before my sons were born, the one role I eagerly awaited was motherhood. The man I chose to father my sons adversely affected the joy of being their mother.

My grandchildren were born during the first years of my marriage to James a relationship which lacked affection and companionship. They were the reason I survived and filled me with joy, empowerment, hope and love. Their love and commitment to me filled the holes in my heart. They attended church events with me as permanent parts of the church family, loved by all. They provided interest and help in my role as pastor, such as folding bulletins, cleaning my office, decorating the church or participating in the service.

Even today as adults, they shower me with loving respect. Each one of my grandchildren is special, possessing kind and gentle spirits.

The Joy of Grandchildren

I am grateful for the memories and honored to be called their Grandma.

Freedom and Voice

From the beginning of my life the Spirit intended to use me to the glory of God. However, my journey followed a path of bumps, detours, break-downs, pot holes, road blocks, crashes, blow-ups, and travel delays.

Feeling abandoned at times, I forgot my heritage as a child of God and that my life had a specific purpose. Yet every time I wandered off the path, God claimed me and reeled me into His presence.

"How could you have been a pastor?" my new neighbor asked me. "You're divorced."

Shocked at her bluntness, I didn't try to defend my marital status or profession as I would have in the past. It did make me stop and think. With my personal life swirling around me, how could I have been an effective pastor?

"I have lived a lot of life," I would say at the first service of every new church appointment. I never claimed to my congregations that I had lived a perfect life but rather I could identify with their lives.

"There isn't anything you have gone through that I would fail to understand," I would continue.

God had given me gifts and talents to use in His kingdom here on earth so before every church service, meeting or activity, I turned my will over to God's will. The Spirit of God would empower me to bypass the guilt and unworthiness so I could be of use in the real world of my church family. This allowed me to be an effective pastor.

As I tell my story I now have justice. My life has a voice, and I have the power to be the person God called me to be. It is my hope that others with similar lives still confined may be inspired to claim the freedom of their voice as well.

The most amazing part of my long and varied journey is that God remained faithful to me.

God was faithful
- when I was not.
- when I sinned.
- when I begged to die.
- when I was unworthy.
- when shame filled me.
- when I felt guilty.
- when grief broke my heart.
- when I failed as a mother.
- when I lost every monetary thing.
- when I faced death.
- when my physical body and spiritual being was broken.

God was faithful in spite of how my ministry ended as a broken, deteriorated, and fragile servant. I thought the curtain was down because I did not know the best was yet to come.

The Divine Spirit empowered me as I sought change and a new direction in my life. Letting go of the shame, forgiving and loving myself has lavished me with this incredible freedom. I now have the power to seek a transformed life of peace and joy. God never abused, abandoned, or rejected me, but taught me the true meaning of what I sought all my life - the amazing unconditional love of God. Writing my life's story gave me voice, and I am grateful for the Spirit's power as I claim my freedom. I want others to claim that same freedom and voice. I believe it is what God wants for everyone.

What Is God's Will for Us?

For those who have been a victim, God offers survival.

What do we think when we hear the word victim? For me my immediate thought is a victim of domestic abuse. Domestic abuse happens when one person chooses to express power and control over another person and it comes in many sizes and shapes.

Just as I failed for many years to realize that the behavior of my previous husbands was abusive, many women think they have no choice but to be treated with disrespect. And like me, many women have distinct spiritual beliefs. We believe that our spouse has the power to lead the family and that God will heal this area of his life.

I believed it was beyond my partners' ability to change. That allowed me to excuse their behavior even when it was physically abusing me, emotionally denying me of my voice, or holding me sexual prisoner. Most of all, I blamed myself by saying there must be something wrong with me.

What I failed to know was that my spouses learned this abusive behavior and they continued because I never held them accountable for it. I never said, "I refuse to live like this anymore. Either we work on changing this behavior, or I can no longer remain with you."

Without holding my previous husbands accountable for their behavior, I remained a hostage without power. I gave them the right to treat me in this manner by remaining loyal to them and defending them to others.

"Whatever you want, dear, is fine with me," I said as I tried to please the person who controlled my life.

"I agree with you. It is my fault," I said in fear even when it was not. I gave them control to rob me of the freedom to voice my opinions.

I am not alone. It happens more frequently than society and the church would like to admit.

According to the National Resource Center on Domestic Violence (NRCDV), three to four million women in the United States are battered every year. The Michigan Resource Center on Domestic and Sexual Violence says that a woman dies from domestic violence in Michigan every six days.

Young and non-informed in my marriage to Andrew, I did not understand the many shapes and sizes of abuse. I had heard of women who were shot, stabbed, or beaten to death. Nevertheless, I believed that would never happen to me.

But I was slapped, punched, choked, smothered, shoved, pushed, kicked, thrown, and burned. My head was beaten against a wall, and I was hit with an object. My husband convinced me I deserved such treatment or denied that it had even happened.

I never thought that forced anal sex, sexual relations with others, or intercourse was abuse. I misunderstood scripture from *I Corinthians 7.4*, which says, *For the wife does not have authority over her own body, but the husband does; likewise the husband does not have authority over his own body.* This scripture written by the apostle Paul was misused. I looked at this scripture as being the Law but God

What Is God's Will for Us?

did not want women disrespected as sex objects and used for the lustful desires of a man.

Marital rape is often laughed at by men who look at the act as an excuse to refuse the husband's advances for sex and claim sex is the man's privilege. Yet, it happens in one of eight marriages.

For me, intimidation was the beginning of abuse that escalated. Yet emotional abuse can be life altering even if it does not become physical. Humiliation, name-calling, and being told I was crazy controlled me. Most of all, threatening behavior such as smashing things or destroying my property, forced me to be treated like a servant.

In my marriage to Lee, as I struggled to gain my voice, I was denied the validation of my ideas and feelings. Lee physically abandoned his family and it victimized us.

When James did not emotionally support me through my difficult adjustment following my bi-lateral mastectomy, I felt abandoned. I needed his affirmation. His rejection for 18 years has had long-term effects on my self-image.

There are so many forms of abuse. My experiences taught me that abuse is not a character defect, a sign of mental illness, or caused by stress. My abusers chose to treat me with physical, emotional, or sexual abuse. They did this because it worked for them and in each case they were accountable for their behavior which could have been unlearned if they had decided to change.

"You deserved it," I was told. I did not provoke the disrespect of abusive behavior because no one and nothing justifies abuse.

From experience, I know that leaving an abusive marriage is a complex process. A victim leaves her abuser anywhere from four to seven times, before she stays safe from her batterer on a permanent basis.

It took me twice to leave before I gained enough confidence to choose permanent safety for my family. It was God's will we would survive. It remains God's will for every woman and child to be safe.

I believe in the power of prayer, but for victims of abuse, praying is not enough. Our connection to the spirit of God is not a passive relationship. In other words, we cannot just sit down, do nothing and expect God to take care of us. Victims need a human being who serves as God's representative who understands the dynamics of abuse and can brainstorm options and resources for a transition to a stable life.

One of the most important resources for any woman is a relationship with another woman as her true friend. This is especially true for women who have been abused and thus not valued or respected by the male gender. Battered women lose their true selves because they fight rejection by 'acting' in another role forced by their abuser. An unconditional friend allows a woman's true self to emerge.

According to the statistics from the NRCDV, sixty-two percent of women who reported they had been in abusive relationships said that having the support of a loving friend or family member helped them get through the relationship safely.

"I would rather have her dead than to let her go," a batterer once said to me. Too many lives of domestic violence victims have been murdered when they have attempted to leave their abusers.

What Is God's Will for Us?

Every measure of safety must be observed. When driving, I was aware and looked in my rear view mirror often. I slept with a knife under my pillow. Filing for divorce was a life and death turning point in my life.

We are God's precious creations with bodies, minds and spirits. In scripture, the question is asked: *Do you not know that you are God's temple and that God's Spirit dwells in you? If anyone destroys God's temple, God will destroy him. For God's temple is holy, and you are that temple. I Corinthians 3:16-17.* Our temples are to be used to the glory of God. It is obvious that God demands us to respect our own temple as well as the temples of others as sacred.

Jesus said *The thief comes to steal and kill and destroy. I came that they may have life and have it abundantly. John 10:10.* Some people come into our lives and they hurt and destroy us. This is not what Jesus wants. Jesus wants us to know the fullness of life so we may feel safe and happy.

My children and I did not deserve to be abused. God did not send us this abuse as punishment and it was not God's will for us to be treated this way.

Abuse is not God's will for anyone. If you are a battered woman and need help, contact a shelter or your pastor. Find someone you can trust. But whatever you do, make it a priority to seek safety. Do not live a victim's life another day. Become a survivor.

For those who have survived, God offers a life that can thrive.

I am a survivor, and proud of it.

Shame Shame Go Away!

I survived my first abusive marriage. I survived the abandonment of my second marriage. I survived the rejection for the love I desperately needed in my third marriage.

Every abuse, abandonment, or rejection left some trauma in my life and each time I failed to deal with its effects. As in the case with many victims, I suffered from depression, anxiety, ulcers, tension, stress, and migraine headaches. I also had a constant desire to hurt myself. Most of all, shame controlled my life. I possessed self-hatred, and lacked the ability to forgive myself.

I allowed my marriages to wrong men to alter my life for so long that I lacked the ability to experience hope, peace, joy, and the love God wanted for me until I sought a journey towards freedom.

Thirty years after I became a survivor for the first time, I became open to the Spirit of God within me that said, 'Surviving is not enough.' These words were laid on my heart when I realized I would rather join the rest of my family in death than to continue living without peace, joy, freedom, and unconditional self-love.

Since the Divine lives within me, I am holy. I am wonderfully made. God expects much more from me than living a joyless life. Living in the past did not give me joy. Pretending my past never happened did not give me joy. Admitting to myself the failures and triumphs of my past faces the truth and gives me freedom.

Sometimes facing the truth means admitting my past to others. If others chose to criticize or judge me or hold my past against me, it is their business, not mine. My business is to accept God's forgiveness and forgiving myself of my past. It is not my

What Is God's Will for Us?

business to let the inherent peace and joy intended for me be stolen by giving others the power to keep me enslaved in shame.

Peace and joy have eluded me by denying my feelings and needs as I accept the behavior of others. Often I have allowed this to happen because I have not taken the time to look at my values, beliefs, or opinions. I now have an awareness to let go of my need to please others at the cost of not living my truth.

I strive each day to treat myself as a righteous person. A righteous person is not perfect. A righteous person is led by the Spirit within to live the right life every day. The right life includes following the only command told me by Jesus, who showed me the way to live, LOVE GOD AND LOVE OTHERS.

Since the Spirit of God lives within me, I love God by loving myself. I love others because God's Spirit lives within them too. I show love by honoring, respecting, and living with the very best intentions. I do not love by fear, guilt and shame.

I am divinely led but I am also fully human. Just leaving an abusive or disrespectful relationship did not automatically guarantee me a life filled with joy and peace. For life changes, I needed to start down the path of healing.

Refusing to live my life as a prisoner, I committed to a journey toward thriving.

Committed To The Journey

To progress from surviving to thriving, I needed first to ask myself: What kept me from the peaceful and joyful life I desire?

Is it shame, guilt, or blame?

Is it anger, pain or fear?

Is it the inability to accept God's forgiveness or to forgive myself?

Is it hatred of God, others, or myself? What is it?

I had never given thought to why I was sad and lacked joy and peace. Life experiences taught me after seeking relationship after relationship that I could not find contentment. I finally learned that it takes time in solitude and digging deep within your heart and soul to find what is eating inside like a cancer or perhaps a roadblock that keeps you from a journey to heal.

After soul searching, I determined it was three issues for me:

- Shame;
- Inability to forgive myself; and
- Seeking unconditional love from others instead of loving myself.

Realizing that what I had been doing was not bringing me what I needed, wanted, and deserved, I needed disciplines that would empower me to live the abundant life rather than the desire of death.

These are the rituals that I use to discipline myself in my healing journey:

Committed To The Journey

1. Acknowledge first that God gave me a Spirit. This Spirit lives within me, and is sacred and holy. All of my religious life, the Spirit of God existed for me, but not inside of me. Ironically, as I baptized individuals, from infant through the age of 90, I said the words, "The Spirit of God lives within you. Live it." Yet I believed that I was not worthy for the Spirit to live within me. I was so disconnected from my Spirit that I refused the idea that it actually existed within me. Therefore, I began a quest of inviting the Spirit, every morning and night to live within my being.

I ask the Spirit to lead me, love me, and guide me. Sometimes I use the form of singing to the Spirit, speaking to the Spirit, or meditating to the Spirit. The most important result is connecting with my Spirit. Since the Spirit of God lives within me, I am empowered to overcome anything. So whatever issue it is for me, after the song, prayer or meditation, every morning, I say whatever is forefront in my heart and mind at that moment:

"Spirit, please help me forgive myself."

"Spirit, please help me let go of my anger."

"Spirit, please help me love myself."

Whatever the issue, I ask every day and several times repeatedly, or several times a day if needed.

2. I write prayers on index cards and keep them on my refrigerator, by my bedside, or my computer table. Some examples are:

Today, dear Lord, I am liberated from my past. I forgive myself for allowing others to disrespect me. A fantastic future awaits me. I will not allow anyone to rob me of it. My eyes, mind, heart and soul have been opened to the truth. I embrace my life completely. For I am love.

Alternatively, I write a prayer to be used on a day when life seems overwhelming:

Today, I ask you to lighten my heart, to lift my burdens, my worries, my fears, my anxieties, and my grief;

So that I may know and cherish all that I am.

I see it. I feel it. I acknowledge it right now!

3. I take time every day, to read a piece of scripture. I often read in the book of Psalms. They tell the deep feelings of the heart. Psalm 55 is the scripture that is often used to refer to the relationship between a victim and the abuser. Other scriptures are:

When you pass through the waters, I will be with you; and through the rivers, they shall not overwhelm you; when you walk through fire you shall not be burned. For I am the Lord your God. Because you are precious in my sight, and honored, I love you. Do not fear, for I am with you.

I will never leave you nor forsake you. I will never abandon you, says the Lord. I have called you by name, you are mine. - Isaiah 43.1c-3a; 4a; 5a

I have set before you life and death, blessings and curses. Choose life so that you and your descendants may live. -Deuteronomy 30.19

Jesus said to them, *The thief comes only to steal and kill and destroy. I came that they may have life and have it abundantly.* - John 10.10 The thief refers to all who steal from us a thriving life.

4. I purchased a journal with a folder. It was not fancy or expensive. Every day I write in my journal, not just as a diary, but

I record what I am feeling. An example might be: Today I criticized the actions of my friend. I feel I must let her business be her business. Or, I feel exhilarated today. Something beyond happy. Not for any reason, just because I am alive. My life has a future.

5. Every day I write out as many "I" statements as I can. This is part of my folder in a separate notebook. I keep my "I" statements so I can look at them in a week or a month. Some examples are:
* I am trustworthy.
* I am not afraid.
* I am worthy.
* I am forgiven.
* I am forgiving.
* I am a good person.
* I am hope.
* I am love.

Every day I take quiet time to affirm what I am that day. I write out in long hand my "I" statements. I do not write my negative thoughts. I have lived a very negative life, and it is time for positive living. My journey continues toward a life that thrives.

6. I read books that tell of the journeys of women who are survivors of abuse and shame and have overcome their joyless lives. So many authors continue to inspire me on my journey. At the conclusion of this book, I have listed authors and books that inspire me.

7. I highlight specific words, sentences, and paragraphs in these books that have provided incredible support for me. I earmark all of my books so when needed, I can easily refer to these places whenever I need to remind myself where I have been in the past and where I am at the present.

8. I use uplifting music which speaks of the power of loving me, empowering myself, and the presence and role of the Spirit within me. I listen to these C.D.'s in my vehicle, and as I fall asleep at night.

9. I have written positive statements from various authors on index cards and place them in my office, in my vehicle or use them as book marks.
Some such statements are:
We don't ask God for too much; in fact, we ask for too little. Turn to Him for everything. Give everything to God. – Marianne Williamson
The way ahead is clear and free. I give myself permission to move out of the past with gratitude and into a joyous new day. – Louise L. Hay
I am an instrument of God's healing love. – Alan Cohen
Loving everything about yourself—even the unacceptable—is an act of personal power. It is the beginning of healing. – Christine Northrup, M.D.
What other people think of me is none of my business. – Dr. Wayne Dyer

10. Every day – sometimes several times a day – I purposefully breathe. I take in deep breaths, letting in the goodness of God, and force my breath out with an 'Ah' that dispels the

Committed To The Journey

negatives forces within me. I will frequently tell myself to breathe. It relieves the anxiety I do not know I have until it is released.

11. I have a spiritual partner who understood the numerous times I fell in the pit and understands the journey I am on. It is someone who reminds me to breathe and reminds me that I am worthy of self-love. It is someone who holds me accountable to my disciplines.

12. At the end of each day, these are the decisions I make:
- What worked today to keep my thoughts positive?
- What change should I work on so tomorrow can be improved?
- How can I celebrate what has been personally accomplished?

Beginning my new life as a healed and whole woman is a journey I need to begin anew every day. The old insecure person is dead and I am very clear about who I have chosen to be. It is a choice I have made to be free from the shame, blame and pain. It is a choice anyone can make. I live as a different person today and it feels so rewarding. You can live a life of peace and joy too.

There are no time restraints to complete my journey. When the old script reflects the old ways of thinking and feeling, my system defaults to its original message of doubt and helplessness. At these times, I catch myself, inhale the new breath of Spirit and exhale the old demons of shame. I am in control of my thoughts. By sticking to my daily spiritual practices, I continue to change the script of my previous thoughts and feelings. I can live my life as God intended.

Shame Shame Go Away!

I am loved, forgiven, healed, surrendered, and empowered to:

CELEBRATE MY LIFE!!

ADDENDUM TO MEMOIR
Following the publication of this book, Mark suffering from PTSD, dealing with the pain of his abuse, over-dosed. His brother, Michael and I found his body. Michael always felt like he had to protect his brother, and felt as though he was not there for him in death. Eight months following Mark's death, anguishing in this survivor's guilt, Michael also overdosed. Now they both rest in peace in the arms of their Lord, and no longer are in pain from their childhood abuse.

Recommended Reading

The Journey from Abandonment to Healing
Susan Anderson

Healing The Shame That Binds You
John Bradshaw

Love Yourself, Live Your Spirit
Sonia Choquette

Truth Heals
Deborah King

Will I Ever Be Good Enough?
Karyl McBride, Ph.D.

Happy for No Reason
Marci Shimoff

Love for No Reason
Marci Shimoff

Every Day I Pray
Iyanla Vanzant

Faith in the Valley
Iyanla Vanzant

In the Meantime
Iyanla Vanzant

Living Through the Meantime
Iyanla Vanzant

One Day My Soul Just Opened Up
Iyanla Vanzant

Peace from Broken Pieces
Iyanla Vanzant

Tapping the Power Within
Iyanla Vanzant

The Value In The Valley
Iyanla Vanzant

Until Today!
Iyanla Vanzant

Yesterday I Cried
Iyanla Vanzant